BRASSEY'S BOOK OF *The* CRUSADES

Also by **David Miller**

U-Boats: The Illustrated History of the Raiders of the Deep

Samurai Warriors

The Wreck of the Isabella

BRASSEY'S BOOK OF

The
CRUSADES

DAVID MILLER

Brassey's
Washington, D.C.

First published in the United States of America by
Brassey's, Inc.
22841 Quicksilver Drive
Dulles, Virginia 20166

Library of Congress Cataloging-in-Publication Data
Brassey's Book of The Crusades, David Miller

ISBN 1-57488-292-9 (alk paper)

First Edition

10 9 8 7 6 5 7 4 3 2 1

Editor: Ray Bonds
Designer: Interprep Ltd
Illustrations: Peter Newark's Military Pictures, except for
maps and diagrams on pages 11, 20, 22, 34, 69, 70, 71, 73
(top), 74, 77, 94, 97, 99 and 102 , which were prepared
by Terry Hadler, and the artworks on pages 54, 57 and 61,
which are reproduced courtesy of Osprey Publishing Ltd.

Printed in Singapore on acid-free paper that meets the
American National Standards Institute Z39-48 Standard.

THE AUTHOR

David Miller is a former British Army officer, who spent his
service in England, the Falkland Islands, Germany, Malaysia,
the Netherlands, Scotland, and Singapore. He subsequently
worked as a freelance author and for three years as a journalist
for Jane's Information Group. Apart from numerous books on
modern defence topics, he has devoted an increasing amount
of time to research into historical subjects. *The Wreck of the
Isabella* was his first historical book; *Samurai Warriors* was
published by Pegasus Publishing in 2000, and he has also
completed a well-received work on the life of Colonel Sir
William De Lancey, who was wounded at Wellington's side at
the Battle of Waterloo in June 1815.

ADDITIONAL CAPTIONS

Page 1: The popular view in the West of the crusaders was
of heroic, and all-conquering knights fighting a noble and
just war under the flag of Christendom, and dealing out
death and destruction to the saracens, as depicted here.
Some crusaders may indeed have been in that mould, but
in many cases the reality was somewhat different.
Pages 2-3: French crusaders embark at a Mediterranean
port, a scene depicted in a 14th Century manuscript.
Pages 4-5: A crusader triumph depicted in a 12th Century
window in the Abbey of St. Denis, which has since been
destroyed. The scene shows the taking of Nicaea on June
1, 1097, one of the earliest successes of the First Crusade.
Nicaea (modern Iznik, Turkey) was of great strategic
importance since it was the capital of the Anatolian Turks,
through whose territory the crusaders had to pass.
Pages 6-7: "The Vigil", a famous painting by John Pettie,
RA, shows the knightly ideal, as a candidate for
knighthood spends the eve of the ceremony in prayer and
contemplation.

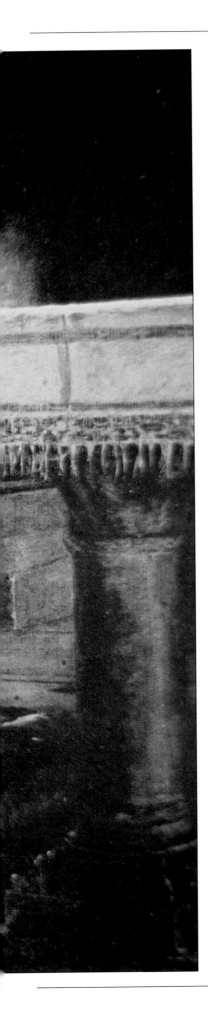

CONTENTS

Introduction

The crusades constitute a clearly defined period in world history when the nations of central, northern, and western Europe combined in a common purpose in order to (as they saw it) free the Holy Land. That period extends from 1096, when the idea of such a crusade was first announced, to 1291, when the last crusaders were driven out of Acre (the present-day Israeli seaport, Akko), their final bastion in the Holy Land. During those two centuries a vast number of people and events were involved and it would require several volumes to cover them in detail, so this book concentrates on the military history of those turbulent times.

The book starts with an overview of the entire period, placing each crusade in its context and identifying the major characters and events involved. This is followed by chapters on three of the most significant military aspects of the crusades. First to be covered are the Military Orders of Knights, which between them contributed so much to the success of the crusades – and also played a major part in their failures. This is followed by a detailed description of the armour and weapons of the crusaders, and then by a survey of one of the most important aspects of the campaigns: fortifications and siege warfare. Three of the most important battles of the period – Hattin, Acre, and Jaffa – are then described in detail and the fact that all three took place in the five years between 1187 and 1192 does not detract from their importance and relevance to the crusades as a whole. Finally, there are a chronology and a glossary of terms.

It is very easy to view some of these events and, in particular, the behaviour of some of the people involved – for example, the killing by forces under King Richard I of the prisoners after the siege of Acre – with strong disapproval. Such judgements are, however, usually made in the context of the morals and values of today, but it must not be forgotten that the crusaders could not know better than to act in the light of the morality of their era. This is not to excuse such acts, many of which were brutal in the extreme and some of which were condemned at the time, but rather to suggest that the environment in which the people were living and the pressures of outside events should be considered before the perpetrators are judged.

This book is a military history of the crusades, a conflict, which involved two of the world's great religions – Christianity and Islam – but the author seeks to make no religious, moral or political judgements about the motives or conduct of either side. This is of particular importance in the choice of terminology, since, as happens in many historical episodes, a variety of terms can be used to describe various aspects of the people and events, some of which appear judgmental, and which can cause confusion, complications or offence. To avoid this, three neutral terms are used throughout this book, as follows:

- The people who conducted the crusades came from central, northern and western Europe, and from a wide variety of nations. They were sometimes referred to as "Latins", because they followed the Roman Catholic rite and the term served to distinguish them from those who followed the Greek Orthodox rites, who were termed "Greeks" (although few were what would be described today as of Greek nationality). The people of the Middle East generally referred to them as "Franks", a term which had been used for several centuries to describe people from western Europe. They are also sometimes referred to as "Christians", since that was the religion which united them in a common purpose. In this book, however, one term only – "crusaders" – is used, which simply describes the undertaking they were involved in.

- The opponents of the crusaders were an amalgam of Arabs, Egyptians, Syrians, Turks, and other Middle Eastern ethnic groups, united by their common religious faith – Islam. These, too, can be described by a variety of terms – by their race, or collectively as "infidels", the term the crusaders used, or by their religion as "Muslims". In this book they are referred to throughout by the term most commonly used by the crusaders themselves – "saracens" – which was derived from the Greek word *sarakênos*, which simply meant "easterner".

- The territory that was the crusaders' destination was, at that time, a geographical approximation rather than a political entity and can be described by a variety of terms. "Palestine" is a historical term which includes what is today Egypt, the State of Israel, the Israeli-occupied Territories, Jordan, Lebanon, and (perhaps) Syria. Another term is "the *Levant*" which covers the territories on the eastern Mediterranean littoral and was derived from the French term levant, meaning sunrise – simply, the area from which the sun rose (as seen from France) and thus, generally, the east. During the crusading period the territory was also known as *outremer*, another French term, which meant "beyond the sea". Then, once the crusaders had established themselves, the territory was split into the Kingdom of Jerusalem and various principalities and counties. In this book, however, the term "Holy Land" is used since it was a territory of great religious significance to both Christianity and Islam.

Chapter 1

THE HISTORY OF THE CRUSADES

The crusades were a series of European military expeditions undertaken in the name of Christianity in general and of the Roman Catholic Church in particular between 1095 and 1270. The geographical area of Palestine, known to the Christians as the "Holy Land" had passed under saracen control and the aim of the crusades was to recover the Christian places of pilgrimage, such as Bethlehem and Nazareth, and, in particular, the holiest site of them all, Jerusalem.

The crusades represent the golden age of chivalry and to the people of western and northern Europe of the time the crusaders were the epitome of knightly perfection. Such men swore a solemn oath either direct to the Pope or to one of his legates and were then presented with a symbolic crucifix in a ceremony known as "taking the Cross". They were then regarded as "warriors of the church" and wore a red cloth cross on their outer garment to symbolise their status. The word "crusade" came from the Latin word *crux*, meaning cross, and so successful was the term as a rallying cry that during the 13th Century the name came to be applied generally to Christian wars against non-Christians, such as pagans, or against Christian heretics, such as the Cathars (Albigensians).

THE BACKGROUND TO THE CRUSADES
Despite the length and difficulties of the journey, by the middle of the 11th Century there was a long tradition of pilgrimage to the Holy Land, by people whose greatest aim in life was, quite simply, to view the Holy Sepulchre

before they died. There were several well-established routes and, as well as princes, nobles, bishops and knights who undertook the pilgrimage, there were an increasing number of humbler men and women who were also taking part; in 1026, for example, a French abbot led some 700 pilgrims to the Holy Land. Thus, while the journey to and from the Middle East was long and dangerous, it was by no means untrodden by people from western Europe.

During the middle of the 11th Century, however, the Christians of western Europe began to take alarm at reports of upheaval in eastern Europe and the Middle East resulting from the expansion of the Seljuk Turks, the latter's conquest of Syria and Palestine causing particular concern. Then, in 1071 the Seljuk Turks took Jerusalem from the Fatimid caliphs of Cairo and totally defeated the Byzantine general, Romanos Diogenes, at the Battle of Mazikert (August 19, 1071). Other Turkish invaders also penetrated deep into the Christian Byzantine Empire and brought many Armenian, Greek, and Syrian Christians under their rule. Then, to top all this, the Turks started to persecute the Christian pilgrims on their way to and from Jerusalem.

Few political events are ever as simple as they appear on the surface and this applies as much to the crusades as to most other events in history. It is certainly true that the great majority of people who went on them did so out of religious conviction and that they were inspired by the great goal of restoring Christian control over the Holy Land. However, other factors were also at work and the crusades offered an outlet for the ambitions of land-hungry knights and noblemen, while the various expeditions offered rich commercial opportunities to the merchants of Italian cities such as Genoa, Pisa, and Venice. Finally, they proved to be a device by which ambitious popes sought to extend their political and religious power, and the crusading armies became, albeit in an indirect sense, the military arm of papal policy.

LEFT: A crusader knight stops to pray at a wayside crucifix on the way to the Holy Land.

RIGHT: The crusaders' goal: the Holy Land as it was in the early 12th Century.

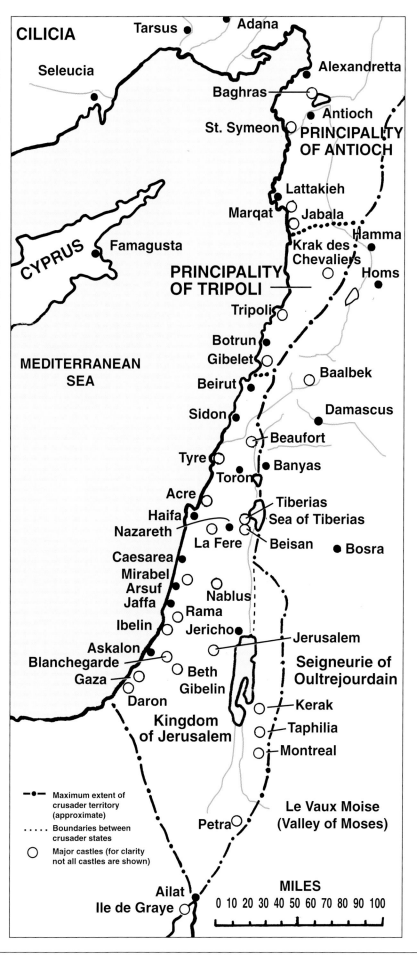

THE BYZANTINE EMPIRE

The Byzantine Empire, which finally disappeared in 1453, featured prominently in most of the crusades. Its name was derived from the original name of the capital city, Byzantium. To its inhabitants at the time, however, it was known as the "Roman Empire" and they regarded themselves as "Romans". The territory it covered was originally the eastern part of the Roman Empire, with its major administrative centre at Byzantium, but when the eastern empire separated from the western part and the city was rebuilt to become the capital by the Emperor Constantine the Great in 330AD it was renamed after him, becoming Constantinople.

At its largest in the 4th Century, this eastern empire stretched from Italy across the Balkans and present-day Greece to Turkey, thence down through Syria, Lebanon, Palestine and Egypt, and finally along the northern coast of Africa to include most of modern Libya. It was vast in scope and very wealthy, with Constantinople becoming the greatest, most opulent and most admired capital city in the world.

Like most empires, it over-reached itself, and in the 5th and 6th Centuries it began to suffer from incursions, losing most of Italy and the Balkans, and coming under increasing pressure from the Persians in the east. Then, in the 7th Century, Islam arose as both a religious and military force and under its inspiration Arabs wrested Egypt, Palestine and Syria from Byzantine control.

In the 9th Century, however, Byzantium carried out a fundamental reorganisation of its civil and military structure, which enabled it to begin to fight back and regain some of the lost territory. Bulgaria was reconquered, and Anatolia and the northern Levant recovered, reaching a high point under the Emperor Basil II. He ruled from 976 to 1025, and led the conquest of Armenia in the east and the destruction of Bulgarian power in the north.

Then, in the middle of the 11th Century, Byzantine power began to wane again. It lost its last remaining territories in Italy, while the Seljuk Turks made increasingly serious inroads in Anatolia, the very heartland of the empire, culminating in their victory over the imperial army at the Battle of Manzikert in 1071.

An added difficulty was caused by the schism between the Greek Orthodox and Roman Catholic Churches, which had been approaching for some time, but finally came about in 1054. Despite that schism, Emperor Alexius I appealed to the Pope for aid against the Turks and the Pope responded with the idea of the crusades. It should be noted, however, that while the primary aim of the Byzantines was to recover lost territory, mainly in Anatolia and the northern Levant, the primary aim of the crusaders was to recover the Holy Land for the Roman Catholic Church.

When they did arrive, the crusaders proved to be a mixed blessing for the Byzantine Empire, as one ill-disciplined army after another straggled across its territory. The imperial authorities seem, wherever possible, to have been reasonably helpful to the crusaders and they provided food and rough accommodation on numerous occasions. They also provided water transport free of charge to several crusades in order to get the people across the Bosphorus and to encourage their early departure from the vicinity of Constantinople. However, the arrival of many thousands of hungry and footsore western Europeans, most of them lacking in any form of discipline or central control, posed an obvious threat, and when the crusaders overstepped the mark the imperial authorities did not hesitate to use force.

That the Byzantines had been correct in their mistrust of the crusaders was clearly demonstrated in the disgraceful attacks made by the Fourth Crusade in 1204, when Constantinople was sacked, many of its people killed and the imperial rulers deposed. The crusaders established the Latin Kingdom of Constantinople which lasted until 1261 when they were expelled by Emperor Michael VIII Paleologus, who restored Byzantine rule. He and his descendants then ruled the empire until 1453 when the city was captured by the Ottoman Turks and the Byzantine Empire came to an end.

JOINING UP

Men and women became "crusaders" by "taking the Cross", which, at least in the early days, involved two separate ceremonies. The first usually took place at an open-air mass rally, led by priests whose job was to whip up a religious frenzy, climaxing in requests for volunteers to come forward to declare themselves and take the vows of a crusader. Then, at a separate ceremony, the crusader would take the vows of a pilgrim, which involved receiving a symbolic purse and staff, as well as a blessing. These vows, it should be noted, normally named a specified period, which could be as much as two to three years.

The crusader's new status was symbolised by wearing a cloth surcoat with a cross on the front and back, the whole symbolising the words of the Bible, "If any man will come after me, let him deny himself and take up his cross and follow me." (Matthew; Chapter 19; Verse 29.) It should be noted, however, that the modern-day picture of a white cloth with a red cross was by no means universal and from about 1150 onwards different colours were used to designate different contingents, with the English wearing white crosses, the Flemish green, French red, and so on.

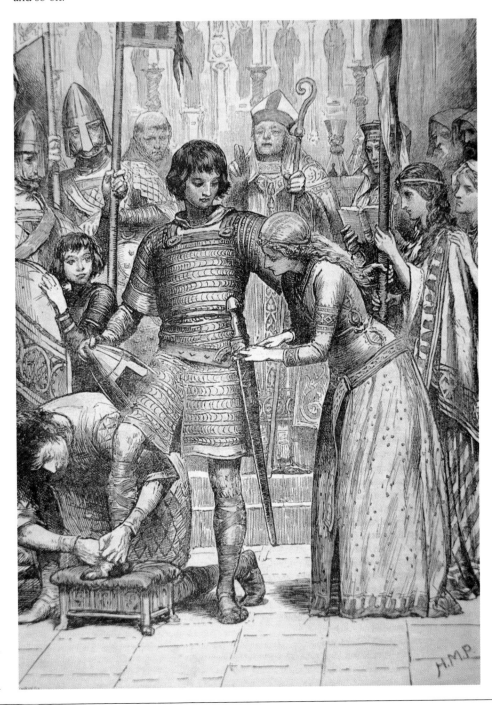

LEFT: Entry of the crusaders into Constantinople (Istanbul) in 1204, during the Fourth Crusade, from a painting by Delacroix.

RIGHT: A newly sworn knight receives a blessing from the bishop. The young man has his helmet in his hand, while his sword is buckled on and his spurs are fastened in place.

By papal decree, crusaders received a number of benefits, some of which were legal and included family and goods being protected by the Church. There was also a moratorium on court proceedings against the crusader during his absence, so that pending cases were either speeded up to enable them to be settled prior to his departure or held over until his return. Similarly, the repayments of debts and imposition of interest were also suspended. In the religious sphere the benefits included release from excommunication, the granting of indulgences, remission of all penances, and the right to have a personal confessor. In many cases, particularly in the latter part of the period, the church also helped to fund poorer knights' crusades from its very considerable wealth.

There was, of course, a scurrilous but relatively small minority who took the vows and wore the cross, but who then avoided undertaking the rigours and dangers of an actual campaign. There were periodic attempts to shame such people into keeping to their vows, usually to little effect, although it did work in the case of the Holy Roman Emperor, Frederick II. He took his crusader vows in 1215, but found a succession of excuses to prevent actually setting out, which made the Pope increasingly frustrated until in 1226 he actually excommunicated him. It clearly had some effect, since Frederick departed for the Holy Land in the following year.

Thus, crusading had a broad appeal to numerous Europeans, although individual motives were very varied. Most went in a state of religious fervour and all knew that their campaign had the Pope's blessing, which gave it not only a gloss of respectability but, whatever else happened, also ensured that they were virtually guaranteed personal salvation. Some went to escape poverty, hardship or other difficulties at home; some went out of greed to see what they could obtain by pillage, and some undoubtedly went out of a simple sense of adventure.

THE FIRST CRUSADE (1097-1099)

Although the idea had been under discussion in general terms for some time, the public origin of the First Crusade can be pinpointed with great precision to an event during the Synod of Clermont in 1095. As part of the synod (church council), Pope Urban II gave a sermon in a field just outside the walls of the French city of Clermont Ferrand on Tuesday, November 27, 1095, to a congregation of clergy and lay-people. During this he outlined his plan for a crusade and called on his listeners to join its ranks. The response was overwhelmingly positive and, in view of this, Urban tasked the bishops attending the council to return home to enlist more volunteers for the Crusade.

Urban had clearly thought everything through, since the strategic plan which he imparted to the bishops before they returned to their sees proved to be very effective. He instructed that groups of crusaders should be assembled, each of which would be responsible to its own leader and would be self-financing, and thus, as much as possible, avoiding any expense on the church. These groups would then start their journey in August 1096 and would make their own way across western Europe to the Byzantine capital, Constantinople (now Istanbul). Once there, the groups would coalesce into a formidable army and then, in conjunction with the Byzantine emperor and his army, they would drive the Seljuk Turks out of Anatolia and push forwards, through Syria and Palestine, until they reached their ultimate goal, Jerusalem.

THE CRUSADE

In general terms, the First Crusade followed Urban's plan, with vigorous recruiting during the remainder of 1095 and the early months of 1096. As a result, four large armies assembled in August 1096 and made their separate ways across Europe to the Byzantine capital at Constantinople.

The first to arrive was a group composed of people from Lorraine, Germany, and northern France, under the leadership of Godfrey de Bouillon, Duke of Lower Lorraine. This group followed the Danube through Hungary and Serbia and on into Bulgaria, where it turned south and crossed the mountains to reach Constantinople on December 23, 1096.

The second to reach the Byzantine capital was actually the last to start. This consisted of Normans from southern Italy who had been inspired by crusaders passing through their territory en route to the Holy Land. These men embarked for Epirus under Duke Bohemond of Otranto and Count Tancred, and then crossed Byzantine territory to arrive in Constantinople on April 26, 1097.

THE EIGHT CRUSADES

CRUSADE	YEARS	AIM(S)	CRUSADER LEADERS	MAIN OPPONENTS	OUTCOME
First	1097-1099	To conquer the Holy Land	Duke Godfrey of Lorraine Baldwin of Lorraine Count Raymond of Toulouse Count Stephen of Blois Count Bohemond of Otranto Count Tancred of Otranto	Sultan Kijid Arslan Emir Kerbhoga of Mosul	Went to Holy Land via Constantinople Crusaders took Antioch, Edessa. Took Jerusalem, July 15, 1099. Success.
Second	1145-1448	To recapture the Holy Land	King Conrad III of Germany King Louis VII of France King Baldwin II of Jerusalem	Muin ed-Din Anar	Crusader defeat. Complete failure.
Third	1189-1192	To recapture the Holy Land	King Richard I of England Holy Roman Emperor Friedrick Barbarossa King Philip II of France King Guy of Jerusalem	Saladin	Crusaders defeated at at Hattin, 1187. Guy laid sige to Acre, 1189. Richard took Acre, 1192. Crusaders could not take Jerusalem. Richard negotiated peace with Saladin. Partial success.
Fourth	1202-1204	To defeat saracens in Egypt To capture Constantinople	Count Theobald of Champagne Count Baldwin of Flanders	Emperor Alexius III of Byzantium	Switched from attack on Egypt to attack on Christian Byzantium. Byzantium captured and sacked. In terms of crusader aims in the Holy Land, a total failure.
Fifth	1218-1221	To establish secure base in Egypt	King John of Jerusalem Papal legate, Cardinal Pelagius	Sultan of Egypt	Took Damietta. Tried to take Mansurah, but were defeated. Complete failure.
Sixth	1228-1229	To recapture the Holy Land	Friedrick II, Holy Roman Emperor	Sultan of Egypt	Friedrich made 10-year treaty which regained Jerusalem plus corridor to the coast. A diplomatic success.
Seventh	1248-1254	To capture base in Egypt To regain Holy Land from the south	King Louis IX of France	Sultan of Egypt	Landed in Egypt in 1249. Captured Damietta, but defeated at Mansurah. Louis captured and ransomed. Complete failure.
Eighth	1270-1272	To convert Bey of Tunis to Christianity To proceed to Holy Land to recapture holy places	King Louis IX of France King Charles of Sicily Prince Edward of England	Bey of Tunis Beybars, Sultan of Egypt	Expedition reached Tunis, but Louis died and crusaders returned home. Complete failure.

ABOVE: The leaders of the First Crusade: (from left to right) Godfrey de Bouillon, Duke of Lower Lorraine; Baldwin, his brother; Raymond of Toulouse; and Bohemond of Tarentum.

The third group on the scene came from southern France, under the leadership of Count Raymond of Toulouse and Bishop Adhemar du Puy. These men fought their way through the Alps then down through Slavonia to the Adriatic, where they followed the Dalmatian coast until they came to a point where they could strike east towards Constantinople, which was reached at the end of April 1097.

The last of these four groups to reach Constantinople was composed of Frenchmen, Normans, and some Englishmen under the leadership of Duke Hugh de Vermandois (the

brother of the King of France), Duke Robert Court-Heuse of Normandy, and Count Stephen of Blois. This group crossed the Alps and then went down through Italy, where they spent the winter, although Duke Hugh went ahead and, despite being shipwrecked, managed to reach Constantinople. The remainder waited until spring and then sailed from the ports of Apulia on the Italian coast to Dyracchium (now Durazzo in present-day Albania), from whence they followed the Via Egnatia to reach Constantinople in May 1097.

THE CONQUEST OF ANATOLIA

For all of these groups, the journey across Europe was by no means uneventful and the impact of the sudden arrival of thousands of travellers on both urban and rural communities in eastern Europe, the Balkans, and Anatolia can only be guessed at. Not surprisingly, the Byzantine emperor, Alexius I Comnenus, and his people found the sudden arrival of these large groups of foreign troops very threatening. Having disposed of the relatively large but militarily unimportant "People's Crusade", Alexius pressed the leaders of the four main groups into agreeing that they would hand over to him any former Byzantine territory that they captured. The crusader leaders did not like these demands at all, which made them deeply suspicious of Byzantine motives, although they all eventually complied.

Their forces complete, the crusaders set off from Constantinople on the next step in their great journey in May 1097. Their first objective was Nicaea (modern Iznik, Turkey) which was then the capital of the Anatolian Turks. When they arrived there, the Byzantine emperor, Alexius, persuaded the garrison to surrender to him rather than to the crusaders, which took place on June 1. This tended to confirm the crusaders' suspicions that they were serving as pawns in Alexius's plans.

Moving on, the crusader army met the main Seljuk Turk field army at Dorylaeum (Eskisehir), where, on July 1, 1097 the crusaders scored their first great victory, almost annihilating the Turkish force. This enabled them to reach the high Anatolian plateau and, despite constant harassment from marauding Turks and excessive heat, they pressed on.

In September the column split, with one group under Tancred and Baldwin of Boulogne leaving the main body to take Tarsus. This group then split again, with Tancred moving into

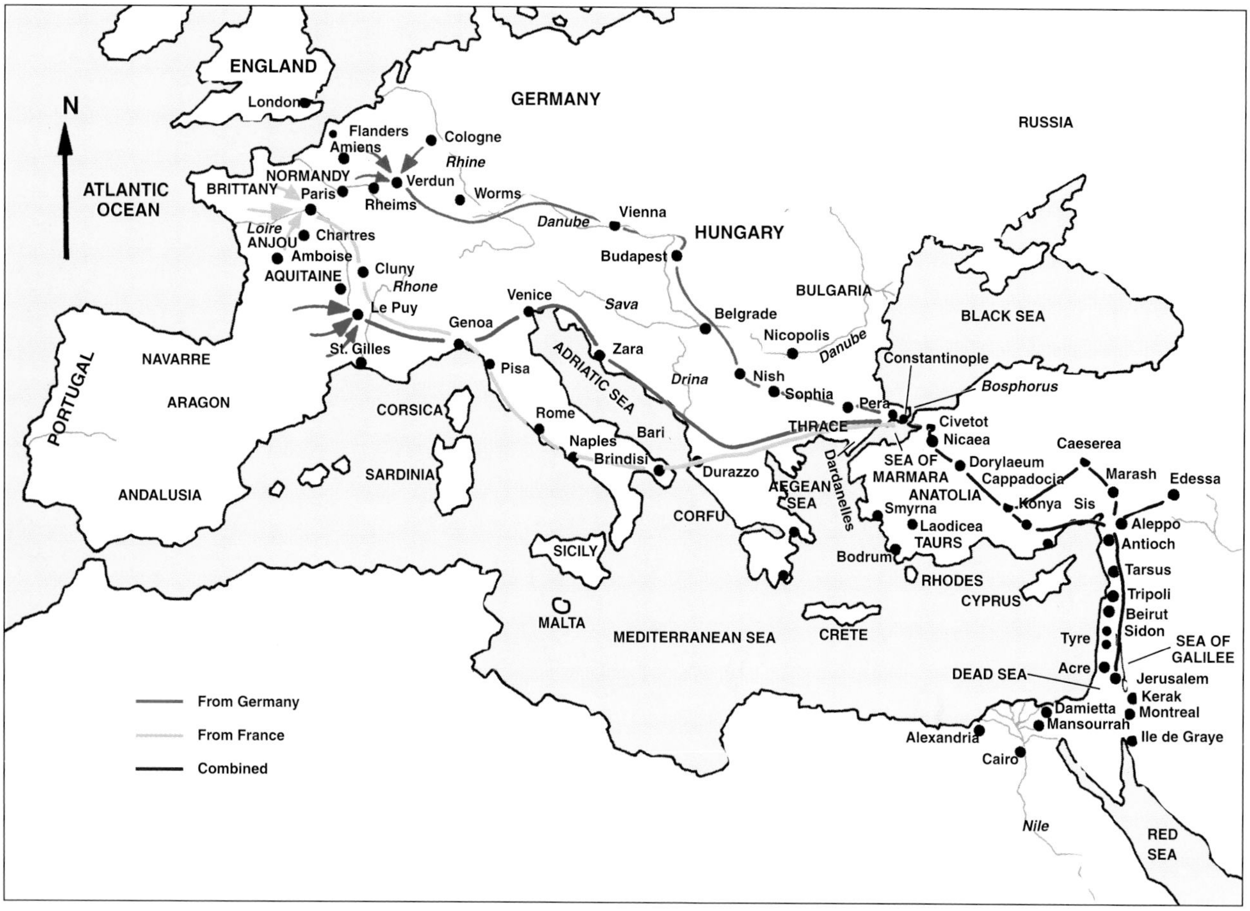

ENGLAND
London
N
GERMANY
RUSSIA
Flanders
Amiens
Cologne
Rhine
ATLANTIC OCEAN
NORMANDY
BRITTANY
Paris
Verdun
Rheims
Worms
Vienna
Loire
ANJOU
Chartres
Danube
HUNGARY
Amboise
Budapest
AQUITAINE
Cluny
Rhone
BULGARIA
Le Puy
Venice
Sava
Belgrade
BLACK SEA
Genoa
Nicopolis
Danube
St. Gilles
Zara
Constantinople
PORTUGAL
NAVARRE
Pisa
ADRIATIC SEA
Drina
Nish
Bosphorus
ARAGON
CORSICA
Sophia
Pera
Rome
Bari
THRACE
Civetot
Nicaea
Naples
Brindisi
Caeserea
SARDINIA
Durazzo
SEA OF MARMARA
Dorylaeum
Cappadocia
Marash
Edessa
ANDALUSIA
AEGEAN SEA
Dardanelles
ANATOLIA
CORFU
Smyrna
Konya
Sis
Laodicea
Aleppo
SICILY
TAURS
Antioch
Bodrum
RHODES
Tarsus
Tripoli
CYPRUS
Beirut
MALTA
MEDITERRANEAN SEA
CRETE
Tyre
Sidon
SEA OF GALILEE
Acre
DEAD SEA
Jerusalem
From Germany
Kerak
Damietta
Montreal
From France
Mansourrah
Alexandria
Ile de Graye
Cairo
Combined
Nile
RED SEA

Celicia, while Baldwin crossed the Euphrates in October and became the Lord of Edessa.

The main body of the crusader army met little resistance during the rest of its campaign in Asia Minor, its next significant obstacle being Antioch, a major coastal city in northern Syria (now Antakya, Turkey). The siege of Antioch started on October 21, 1097, but the city held out for seven months, not falling until June 3 the following year. A large Turkish army was on its way to attack the besieging force, but fortunately for the crusaders they took the city in time to be able to turn and beat the relieving force, which they did on June 28, 1098

ABOVE: The First Crusade (1097- 1099) was a success. In spite of many unforeseen obstacles, the disparate elements managed to reach the Holy Land and to capture Jerusalem, which fell to them on July 15, 1099.

THE CAPTURE OF JERUSALEM

Having taken Antioch, the crusaders rested for a while, not setting out on the next phase of their campaign until late November 1098. Moving slowly, they crossed into the Holy Land in May 1099 and arrived in front of their goal – Jerusalem – on June 7. The slow progress was inevitable with a medieval army but, apart from at Antioch, the crusaders had been relatively uninterrupted, since they had avoided attacking cities and castles in order to conserve their forces.

At this time Jerusalem was under Egyptian control and the garrison was both strong and well prepared for a siege, but the crusaders were also strong, in good heart, and had the ultimate prize literally before their eyes. They were also reinforced by a newly arrived army from Genoa, which brought additional and much needed siege machines. These were duly assembled and after a relatively short siege the crusaders took Jerusalem by storm on July 15. There then followed a disgraceful episode in which the city's gates were closed and every last non-crusader, whether man, woman or child, was massacred on the grounds that this was purifying the Holy City in the blood of the defeated infidels.

A week later the nobles heading the various contingents met and elected one of their number, Godfrey of Bouillon, Duke of Lower Lorraine, as ruler of the newly won city. He was offered, but modestly declined, the title of "king". Then, under Godfrey's command, this particular army then fought its last campaign, defeating an advancing Egyptian army at Ascalon (now Ashqelon, Israel) on August 12. Shortly afterwards the great majority of the

RIGHT: It is almost impossible to imagine the joy which the crusaders felt when they came within sight of the Holy City – the goal towards which they had been struggling for two long and hard years.

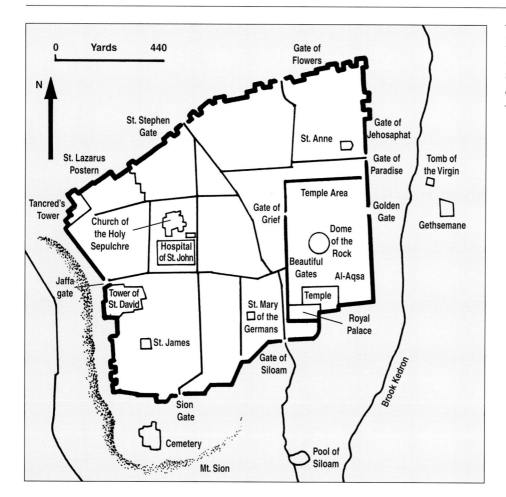

crusaders, their task achieved, departed homewards, leaving Godfrey with a relatively small number of men to maintain control over the conquered territories.

THE HIGH TIDE OF CRUSADER POWER IN THE EAST

As a result of their successes in the First Crusade, the crusaders had changed the map of the Middle East and had established four states. At the head was the King of Jerusalem to whom the others, at least in theory, paid tribute, although in practice there were many disagreements and quarrels.

ANTIOCH

The northernmost and the first of the crusader states to be established was the Principality of Antioch, centred on the Orontes Valley and the very wealthy city of Antioch, with a long coastline running from Tarsus in the north to Jabala in the south, and a hinterland stretching to the border with the County of Edessa. When it was captured by the First Crusade in 1098, the city was granted to one of the leaders, Bohemond, a Norman from Apulia in southern Italy (1057-1111). Bohemond was captured by the saracens in 1100, when his nephew Tancred took over as regent until his uncle's return. Bohemond's descendants ruled the principality until 1268.

EDESSA

The second of the crusader states to be established was the County of Edessa, which lay to the east of the Principality of Antioch and whose possession was necessary to protect the crusaders' north-eastern flank. Largely populated by Armenian Christians, it was a somewhat amorphous territory with no natural frontiers and had to be controlled by a network of castles. Edessa's first crusader count, Baldwin I, was appointed King of Jerusalem in 1100 and was succeeded in Edessa by his nephew, Baldwin of Le Bourg. When Baldwin I died in 1118 the nephew was appointed king in his place as Baldwin II, handing over the County of Edessa to Joscelin, whose son succeeded him, but it was lost in 1150, never to return to crusader hands.

BELOW: *The capture of Jerusalem, from a painting by a 14th Century French artist. Note the trebuchet (bottom right) and siege tower; such contemporary pictures of military equipment are rare.*

TRIPOLI

Immediately to the south of the Principality of Antioch lay the much smaller County of Tripoli on the Syrian coast, whose first ruler was Raymond, Count of Toulouse. Raymond conquered all the territory apart from the city itself, and he began the siege in 1104. Raymond died in 1105 and it was not until 1109 that the city finally fell, by which time the title had passed through William-Jordan to Bertrand, who held the title of Count of Tripoli as a vassal of the King of Jerusalem.

JERUSALEM

The largest and most powerful of the crusader states was Jerusalem, whose first ruler, Godfrey, had been elected in 1099 but died the following year. He was succeeded by his brother, Baldwin I, who adopted the title Godfrey had rejected -

King of Jerusalem - which thereafter became hereditary. One problem, which arose on several occasions, was when a king died without a son to inherit the title, but with a daughter. On her father's death the daughter became queen, but the man she married then became king; the marriage of a female heir apparent was therefore a matter of considerable interest.

ABOVE: Duke Godfrey de Bouillon leads his men from the top of the siege tower and onto the walls of Jerusalem. Below him a priest says prayers to ensure success and to encourage the faint-hearted.

SEIGNEURIE OF OULTREJOURDAIN

One of the most important subordinate elements of the Kingdom of Jerusalem was the Seigneurie of Oultrejourdain. This encompassed the crusader territory east of the River Jordan in the territories that were generally known as Idumea and Moab, and which extended, at least in theory, as far south as the port of Äilat at the head of the Gulf of Aqaba. The first lord was Roman de la Puy, appointed in 1115, but his son supported the loser in one of the many crusader quarrels and was dispossessed in 1132, the lordship then being granted to one Pagan the Butler, a court official in Jerusalem. Pagan was a born governor and established a network of castles, which brought his seigneurie under control, including the famous Kerak of Moab. It dominated the only caravan route from the south, including Egypt and Äilat to Damascus in the north, and thus became a fruitful source of tax revenue.

REINFORCEMENTS

When news of the success of the First Crusade reached western Europe it resulted in more crusaders setting out for the Holy Land. Three groups passed through the Byzantine capital of Constantinople in 1101-1102 and then set out to complete their journeys, but all three met similar disasters as they crossed Anatolia. The first group was smashed at Mersevan in 1101, the second and third groups at Heraclea in 1101 and 1102, respectively, and in all three cases only a few escaped.

Two groups of crusaders even came from as far away as Scandinavia. The first, under the

RIGHT: A week after capturing the Holy City, the leaders met and offered the leadership of the new Kingdom of Jerusalem to Duke Godfrey de Bouillon.

Danish king, Eric the Good, followed an overland route through Russia and thence to Cyprus, where Eric died. His wife then took command and continued to Jaffa. In 1107 a Norwegian expedition under Sigurd, one of three brothers sharing the Norwegian throne, sailed from Norway, across the North Sea, through the English Channel and thence down the Atlantic coasts of France, Portugal, and Spain, until they turned eastwards into the Mediterranean, reaching Acre in 1110. Sigurd visited Jerusalem and then helped Baldwin attack Sidon before returning to his distant northern kingdom. This little known episode was one of the great achievements of the crusades, both outward and homeward voyages representing an epic accomplishment in those days.

ABOVE: Christian knights fighting saracen cavalry. On arrival in the Holy Land such knights wore the same type of armour and clothing they would have worn in northern Europe, but they were quickly forced to adapt to the hot climate.

CONSTANT CONFLICT

The victories of the First Crusade had been possible, in large part, to the isolation and relative weakness of the various saracen powers, but the saracen resistance to this invasion continued. The generation following the First Crusade saw constant warfare between the newly established crusader states and their Muslim neighbours, which led to the beginning of Muslim reunification under the leadership of Imad ad-Din-Zangi, ruler of Mosul and Halab (Aleppo), who was generally known as Zangi.

King Baldwin I was almost constantly at war, defending his kingdom against saracen attacks from Egypt. With only 1,100 men, he defeated a 32,000-strong Egyptian army at the First Battle of Ramleh in 1101, but was, in his turn, defeated at the Second Battle of Ramleh in 1102, although he then recovered and defeated the Egyptians at Jaffa, also in 1102.

The campaigns continued with Baldwin marching across Sinai to the Gulf of Aqaba in 1117, where he built a fortress at Äilat. The following year Baldwin set out to conquer Egypt, but he died en route and his army then returned home to Jerusalem. The saracens slowly attained a degree of fusion and in 1144 Zangi led them to their first major victory against the crusaders by taking the city of Edessa, following which he set about the systematic dismantling of the crusader state in that region.

THE SECOND CRUSADE (1147-1149)

The papacy's response to Zangi's successes was to proclaim the Second Crusade late in 1145. The new expedition attracted numerous recruits, among them King Louis VII of

ABOVE: The crusaders proved to be great engineers, one of their finest achievements being the Krak des Chevaliers, shown here in all its glory. The fortress was rebuilt, in the form shown here, by the Knights Hospitallers, but they could not afford the manpower to garrison it properly.

France, and Conrad III, the Holy Roman Emperor. Conrad's German army set out for Jerusalem from Nuremberg, Germany, in May 1147, with Louis and the French forces following about a month later. Louis was accompanied by his redoubtable wife, Eleanor of Aquitaine, who brought a train of several hundred ladies with her.

The German expedition reached Constantinople first, where Conrad was given some excellent advice by Emperor Manuel I Comnenus, who told him to follow the coastal road around Anatolia and to send home the non-combatant pilgrims. Conrad chose to disregard both and travelled straight across Anatolia where his people ran out of food and water, were caught by the Turks, and were massacred at Dorylaeum on October 25, 1147. Only a few survived, Conrad himself being one of them.

The few remnants of the German army managed to join up with the French army at Nicaea and both then followed around the Anatolian coast. On their separate journeys across Europe the French had been much better disciplined than the Germans. However, the discipline of the French forces also deteriorated as their combined column wound its way around the Anatolian coast. After a minor engagement with the Turks, Louis decided to split his force at a small port called Attalia. He then took his court and most of the cavalry to the Holy Land by sea, leaving the balance of the cavalry and all of the infantry to make their own way by road. Shortly afterwards the leaders of the remaining cavalry decided that they did not wish to be left behind, so they, too, took ship leaving the foot soldiers and pilgrims to make their own way. Abandoned by their leaders, these unfortunate people carried on, harassed by the Turks and hampered by disease, sickness, hunger, and exhaustion; fewer than half of those that set out from Attalia reached Antioch in May of the following year.

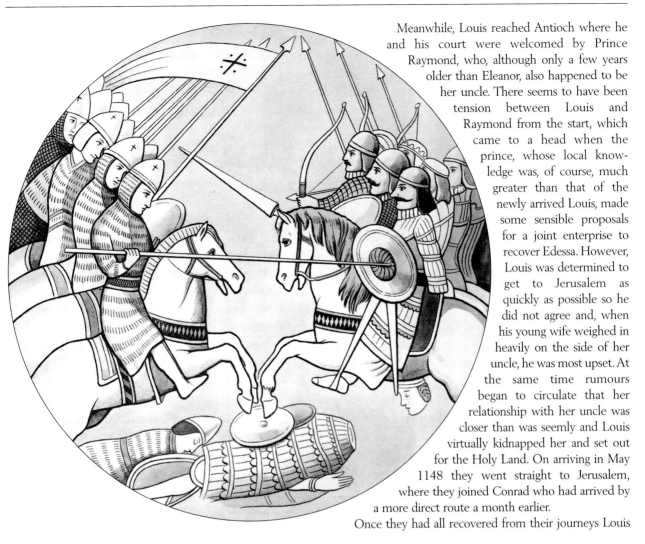

Meanwhile, Louis reached Antioch where he and his court were welcomed by Prince Raymond, who, although only a few years older than Eleanor, also happened to be her uncle. There seems to have been tension between Louis and Raymond from the start, which came to a head when the prince, whose local knowledge was, of course, much greater than that of the newly arrived Louis, made some sensible proposals for a joint enterprise to recover Edessa. However, Louis was determined to get to Jerusalem as quickly as possible so he did not agree and, when his young wife weighed in heavily on the side of her uncle, he was most upset. At the same time rumours began to circulate that her relationship with her uncle was closer than was seemly and Louis virtually kidnapped her and set out for the Holy Land. On arriving in May 1148 they went straight to Jerusalem, where they joined Conrad who had arrived by a more direct route a month earlier.

Once they had all recovered from their journeys Louis

ABOVE: A 12th Century idea of contemporary combat during the crusades. The crusaders are armed with spears, while the saracens carry a mixture of swords, bows and lances.

LEFT: Crusaders pass through the city of Vienna on their way to the Holy Land. Such hordes of poorly organised travellers left a trail of destruction and pillage that stretched across Europe.

RIGHT: Pope Urban II gives his blessing to would-be crusaders in the city of Clermont Ferrand on November 27, 1095. His call to arms met a much stronger response than he had dared hope.

II and Conrad held a meeting with King Baldwin II of Jerusalem where they agreed jointly to attack Damascus. This proved to be a decision of the utmost folly, which resulted in a large and magnificent army being utterly humiliated. The great army arrived outside Damascus on July 24, 1148, and was forced to withdraw just five days later. The crusaders suffered very heavy losses and the leaders, as so often throughout the crusades, fell out, so the French and German kings and the remains of their armies returned home.

THE THIRD CRUSADE (1189-1192)

When the Second Crusade ended in fiasco the Muslim powers were free to resolve their differences with each other. Zangi had died in 1146, but his successor, Nur ad-Din, rapidly expanded the territory under his control and by 1169 had become a major power in the Middle East. His successes culminated in 1169 when his forces, under the command of one of the greatest warriors of the period, Saladin, conquered Egypt. When Nur ad-Din died five years later, Saladin succeeded him to become the ruler of an Islamic state that stretched along the Mediterranean coast from the Libyan Desert through Egypt and then around the Levant to the Tigris Valley, surrounding the crusader states on three fronts.

ABOVE: Frederick I, Barbarossa, embarks for the Third Crusade. He never reached the Holy Land but was drowned in an avoidable accident in an Anatolian river.

RIGHT: An imperious and bearded Frederick I (Barbarossa means "red beard") crosses the Bosphorus. He led a contingent of 30,000 crusaders – a powerful and well-organised army.

ELEANOR OF AQUITAINE (1122-1204)

One of the most extraordinary people of her time was Eleanor of Aquitaine (ca 1122-1204), whose turbulent life included going on the Second Crusade, being first Queen of France and then Queen of England, and later becoming the mother of one of the most beloved of all English kings, Richard the Lionheart. Eleanor's own family background was complicated, to say the least. Her grandfather, Duke William IX of Aquitaine (1070-1127), went on the First Crusade, where he acquitted himself well. Apart from being a warrior, and a rich and powerful ruler, however, he was also a musician and poet, whose colourful court was famous for its elegance and refinement, resulting in his popular title "the Troubadour".

Duke William's personal life was somewhat complicated. His first wife was Ermengarde, whom he divorced and sent to a monastery, following which he married Philippa of Toulouse, the widowed Queen of Aragon. William and Philippa had two sons and three daughters, but he then tired of her, as well, and despatched her to the same monastery as Ermengarde.

The duke's eyes then fell on a married woman, with the rather apt name of Dangereuse, who was the wife of the Viscount de Châtellerault. Duke William abducted her and set her up as his mistress, following which he insisted that his son and heir (by his second wife, Philippa of Toulouse), who was also called William, should marry Aenor, Dangereuse's eldest daughter by her husband, the Viscount de Châtellerault. Despite this complicated background, William (the younger) and Aenor enjoyed a happy marriage and had three children, two girls and one boy, of whom the eldest was a girl, Eleanor.

When Duke William IX died in 1127, his son became Duke William X, but when the latter's wife, Aenor, and their only son died, their eldest daughter, Eleanor, became the heir apparent to the duchy. She was a high-spirited, intelligent and, by every account, very beautiful girl, who, unusually for the time, was given an excellent education and travelled a great deal with her father. Then, when her father died in 1137, the girl, then aged fifteen, inherited the duchy, making her powerful, wealthy, and very eligible, and now with the name by which she is known to history of "Eleanor of Aquitaine".

QUEEN OF FRANCE

On his deathbed Duke William X commended his daughter to the care of the King of France, Louis VI, also known as "the Fat", who promptly married her to his eldest surviving son and heir. Within weeks of the marriage Louis the Fat died, his son succeeding him as Louis VII, so that, at the age of sixteen, Eleanor was now Queen of France. During this marriage it would appear that Louis adored his beautiful and talented wife and that he consulted her often, but he was a quiet and pious man and she was beautiful and full of life, and subsequent events suggest that, although they had two children (one stillborn and a second, a daughter, who did survive), his love was not returned.

SECOND CRUSADE

When Louis decided to go on the Second Crusade, the adventurous Eleanor immediately raised a thousand men from Aquitaine to join his contingent, but on condition that she – and a train of 300 women – should go with them, to which Louis agreed. They eventually arrived in Antioch, which was ruled by Eleanor's uncle, Raymond of Poitier, who had married the ruling princess of that city. It was rumoured that Eleanor had a love affair with her uncle, although whether that was true or not was never proven, but she certainly did take Raymond's side in several arguments with her husband. Their most notable difference of opinion was over the next strategic step in the crusade: Louis wanted to head straight for Jerusalem, while Raymond, supported by Eleanor, wanted to take Edessa first to secure the crusaders' northern flank.

When Louis refused, Eleanor demanded a divorce, at which Louis was both angry and hurt, and he then set out for Jerusalem, taking Eleanor, more or less by force, with him, although she insisted on separate ships. They later visited Rome on their homeward journey, where the Pope persuaded them to resume their conjugal relations, which resulted in their only child to survive to adulthood, a girl named Alix.

QUEEN OF ENGLAND

The marriage between Louis and Eleanor was annulled in 1152 on the pretext of a remote blood kinship, although the real reasons seem to have been a combination of Eleanor's failure to produce a male heir and her desire to escape from what was, at least for her, a loveless marriage. But she retained all her vast estates in Aquitaine and, apart from being very attractive, was also still very eligible. Only eight weeks after the divorce she married Henry Plantagenet (1133-1189), Duke of Normandy and Count of Anjou, who was aged eighteen and thus eleven years younger than his bride. Gossip-mongers always found plenty to say about Eleanor and she gave more fuel to their fires when she gave birth to a son after only five months of marriage. The child died a few years later.

Meanwhile, her husband had become Henry II, King of England, and Eleanor, who had once been Queen of France, was now Queen of England. She gave Henry five sons and three daughters. Henry then started taking mistresses, the most notable being Rosamund Clifford. It was alleged that one night Eleanor confronted her with a poisoned chalice in one hand and a dagger in the other – and offered her husband's mistress the choice! Meanwhile Henry II arranged a marriage between his eldest surviving son, Richard (1157-1199), later to be known as "The Lionheart", and the daughter of Louis VII and his second wife. The girl went to the English court to complete her education, but when Richard ignored his bride-to-be, his father seduced her.

REBELLION AND REGENCY

Towards the end of the 1160s there was trouble in Aquitaine so Eleanor went there to restore order, re-establishing her court at Poitier, which became a great centre of the arts. Then, in 1173, she supported her sons in a revolt against their father, but Henry defeated them and imprisoned Eleanor, who was not released until 1185.

When her husband died in 1189 Eleanor secured the throne for her son, who became King Richard I (1157-1199). He had become heir apparent on the death of his eldest brother in 1183. The new king then departed on the Third Crusade, leaving his mother, Queen Eleanor, as a highly effective regent in his place. Even so, Eleanor found both the time and the energy to escort Berengaria of Navarre all the way to Sicily to meet Richard, whom Berengaria was to marry.

When Richard was killed during a minor skirmish in France in 1199 he was succeeded by his younger brother John (1166-1216). Eleanor then retired to an abbey in France where she died in 1204, aged about 82, a very advanced age for the Middle Ages, after what can only be descibed as an eventful and adventurous life.

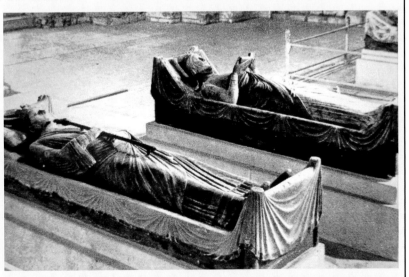

Eager to rid the area of the alien crusaders, Saladin invaded the Kingdom of Jerusalem in May 1187 and on July 4 he inflicted a crushing defeat on the crusader forces at the Battle of Hattin in Galilee, in the aftermath of which he captured many of the crusader strongholds. The Holy City itself surrendered to Saladin on October 2, leaving Tyre as the only major city still in crusader hands.

Once again the bad news from the Holy Land swept through Europe and on October 29, 1187, Pope Gregory VIII announced the Third Crusade. As before, the papal proclamation was greeted with widespread enthusiasm and the three greatest European monarchs of the new generation "took the Cross": Frederick I, the Holy Roman Emperor; King Philip II of France; and King Richard I of England. The English king, who would become known as *Coeur de Lion* (the Lionheart) for his exploits on the crusade, was the son of remarkable parents – King Henry II and the redoubtable Eleanor of Aquitaine – the latter being very much still alive. These kings and their numerous followers constituted the largest crusading force that had taken the field since 1095, but the outcome of all this effort was meagre.

The German contingent, some 30,000 strong, left in the spring of 1189 and marched overland to Constantinople where they spent the winter. In 1190 they continued and repulsed several Turkish attacks, but Frederick was drowned in a rather silly accident in a river in Cilicia and his much less effective son, Friedrich von Schwaben, took over. Some men returned home while others continued to the Holy Land, but the strength of the forces was steadily reduced by starvation, disease and constant harassment by Turkish light cavalry, and only about a thousand arrived at Acre later in the year.

RICHARD THE LIONHEART

The English and French kings, Richard and Philip, started out together a year after Frederick, travelling across France and thence to Sicily where they wintered, devoting most of their time to a constant series of quarrels. As a result they continued their journeys independently, with Philip sailing direct to Acre, while Richard went to Cyprus where he fell out with the local ruler and then conquered the island in May 1191. This happened more or less by accident, but had the advantage of securing the island as a valuable logistic base. Richard then went on to Acre, arriving on June 18 to discover that a major siege was in progress. The dynamic Richard took command by common consent of all except the French, revitalised the army, and led the besieging force to victory only a month later. The terms of the surrender included the payment of a ransom and when this was not forthcoming by August 20, as stipulated, Richard, in one of the incidents which have besmirched the reputation of the crusaders, ordered the massacre of 2,700 saracens, including women and children.

Richard then conducted a masterly advance down the coast, the fleet keeping pace with the marching troops, before he turned inland towards Jerusalem, keeping his army under tight control. Harassed by Saladin's forces, he won a significant victory at the Battle of Arsouf (September 7, 1191). But despite his generalship and logistical preparations, Richard was frustrated by Saladin's scorched earth policy, which resulted in a lack of food for the crusade's people, of fodder for their horses and of water for all, so, unable to recapture Jerusalem, Richard withdrew to the coast.

Saladin was told that Richard was at Acre so he descended on Jaffa in July 1192 and had almost captured it when Richard arrived by ship. There followed a battle in which the balance of advantage swayed between the two sides until Richard was eventually victorious. Richard then made a treaty with Saladin and eventually departed from the Holy Land in October 1192, never to return. The Latin Kingdom which he left was smaller than the original kingdom and considerably weaker, both militarily and economically, but what remained lasted, albeit somewhat precariously, for another century.

THE FOURTH CRUSADE (1202-1204)

In 1199 Pope Innocent III issued yet another summons to Christendom to recover Jerusalem from the saracens, which led to the Fourth Crusade under the leadership of Count Theobald III of Champagne, supported by Count Louis de Bois and Count Baldwin of Flanders. It was agreed that the expedition should assemble at Venice, from whence the Venetians would transport them by sea; it was estimated that some 25,000 men would require transport, for which the price would consist of two elements: an 85,000 marks capital sum and the handing

ABOVE LEFT: Richard I (right, foreground), a consummate general, discusses plans for the Battle of Arsouf (September 7, 1191) with the Master of the Knights Hospitaller, Godfrey de Duisson (left).

LEFT: The major feature of the Third Crusade (1189-92) was the confrontation between Richard I and the saracen leader, Saladin, the two greatest battlefield commanders of their day.

over to the state of Venice of half of all crusader conquests. The original plan was that the expedition would land in Egypt and would then advance along the coast to retake the Holy Land from the south, but when Count Theobald died in May 1201 the Marquis Boniface de Montferrat was elected to take his place. This resulted in a complete change of plan and it was now decided that the expedition would sail to Constantinople instead of Egypt, then cross Anatolia on horse and foot, and then descend on the Holy Land from the north, by what was now the traditional route.

The expedition duly assembled at Venice in the summer of 1202, but the first problem arose when the crusaders could not raise the 85,000 marks lump sum, although the Venetians eventually agreed to take them provided that the crusaders first recovered the city of Zara for Venice. This city was on the Adriatic coast and ruled by the King of Hungary, who was not only a fellow Christian but had also "taken the Cross". When news of the proposed attack on the property of a fellow crusader reached the Pope he threatened the expedition with a

1883.
L. Andriolli

blanket excommunication, but this failed to deter them and the city duly fell on November 24, 1202. The crusaders were immediately excommunicated, although the Pope then relented, lifting the ban on condition that the crusaders did not attack any further Christian property, which is precisely what they now proceeded to do, their next target being the eastern Christian capital at Constantinople.

Having kept their bargain with the Venetian authorities and in spite of the Pope's anger, the crusaders departed aboard the Venetian transports and arrived off Constantinople in June 1203, where the troops disembarked and established a fortified camp ashore. The Venetian fleet then entered the Bosphorus and in a combined land/sea attack Constantinople was taken and a fine of 200,000 marks imposed, following which the crusaders fell back to their camp to await the payment. In January 1204 there was an insurrection by some of the Byzantine nobles who objected to the imposed charge, which led to a very short but extremely violent siege (April 11-13, 1204) at the end of which the crusaders and Venetians took Constantinople and proceeded to loot and sack it with a degree of ruthlessness seldom seen, even in those brutal times. Their immediate hunger for booty assuaged, the crusaders and Venetians next proceeded to establish the Latin Empire of Constantinople, which survived for less than sixty years and contributed nothing to the defence of the Holy Land. Thus, the crusaders of the Fourth Crusade, who had gone to the Middle East to protect Christianity, had succeeded only in hastening the destruction of what had been the real bulwark of Christianity there.

THE FIFTH CRUSADE (1218-1221)

Eleven years passed after this debacle before Pope Innocent III decided to try again, taking the opportunity provided by the Fourth Lateran Council in December 1215 to propose a new crusade. The volunteers, led by King Andrew of Hungary, assembled at the Adriatic port of Split, but recruiting had been so successful that there was insufficient shipping available, and many men returned home. Then when those that did sail arrived at Acre they were too few in number and they were used by the local leaders for a variety of unimportant military tasks, for example, an abortive attack on a saracen encampment on Mount Tabor, until more men arrived.

The expected contingents did arrive in Acre, including groups from Austria, Holland, Hungary, and Scandinavia, but with the notable absence of the French. By this time King Andrew of Hungary had decided that he had fulfilled his vows and had set off for home in January 1218, so John of Brienne, King of Jerusalem, took command and it was agreed to mount an expedition against the Egyptian fortress of Damietta in the Nile Delta. Transported in Italian ships, the crusader army arrived off Damietta in May 1218, where they set up a camp on an island and laid siege to a massive, fortified tower that commanded the approach to Damietta. As at Acre, a floating siege tower was built, supported by two ships lashed together, but on this occasion it was successful and the fortified tower fell three months later.

In September 1218 reinforcements from Italy arrived, led by the Papal legate, Cardinal Pelagius, who immediately insisted on taking responsibility for the overall direction of the crusade, although King John of Jerusalem remained in operational command of the army. The Sultan of Egypt offered to negotiate on a number of occasions, proposing increasingly generous terms, but Pelagius, supported by the leaders of the military orders refused, mainly on the grounds that the Holy Roman Emperor, Frederick II, was supposed to be on his way, and would then exercise effective military command which would doubtless be crowned with success. The siege of Damietta lasted for eighteen months and it eventually fell in November 1219 after both the crusaders on their island and the saracens inside the fortress had been depleted by hunger and disease. Despite this success Pelagius still insisted on waiting and eventually a German army did arrive in early 1221, consisting of two contingents, one from the Teutonic Order and a second led by Louis, Duke of Bavaria, but it was nothing like the size promised, nor was it led by the Emperor Frederick.

So, having wasted no less than twenty months, Cardinal Pelagius ordered the crusaders, now some 46,000 strong, to march on Cairo. Their first objective was a saracen camp at Mansurah and the crusaders set up a camp on a nearby island. But when the Nile waters rose unexpectedly the crusaders were threatened with drowning and were left with no choice but to agree to a treaty under which they lost everything they had gained. As a result the crusade broke up in September 1221 in disillusionment and ignominy.

LEFT: *Grim and determined, crusaders set out on another leg of their long march across Europe, with a crucifix held aloft so that all could see and take inspiration from it. However good their intentions, the reality was that they were an ill-disciplined horde.*

THE SIXTH CRUSADE (1228-1229)

Frederick II, who had failed to arrive in Egypt in 1221, had in fact taken the crusader's oath in 1215 and then renewed it in 1220, but for domestic political reasons (accompanied, perhaps, by a personal reluctance for the rigours of campaigning) kept postponing his departure. Frederick married the thirteen-year-old Yolande, daughter and heir presumptive to King John of Jerusalem, and Frederick then declared himself to be King of Jerusalem, apparently overlooking the fact that his father-in-law was not yet dead. Meanwhile, the Pope was becoming increasingly frustrated by Frederick's failure to fulfil his vow and depart for the Holy Land, but the emperor eventually gave in, sailing from Italy with a large army in August 1227. However, within a few days Frederick was taken ill and insisted that the convoy should return to port, at which point the Pope, outraged at yet another delay, excommunicated the emperor.

ABOVE: A medieval woodcut of Jerusalem gives a feel for the high walls and many towers that surrounded the city.

RIGHT: Another disaster, this time on the Seventh Crusade, as the saracens capture Louis IX, King of France, in March 1250.

Frederick embarked for the Holy Land yet again in June 1228 and this time actually reached his destination, disembarking at Acre later in the year. More disaster quickly followed, however, as most non-German contingents now refused to obey Frederick's orders on the grounds that he had been – and was still – excommunicated. Undeterred, Frederick proceeded to conduct this most unconventional crusade almost entirely by diplomatic negotiations with the Egyptian Sultan Al-Kamil. In these skilfully conducted negotiations Frederick managed to disguise the real weakness of his position and managed to obtain agreement to a peace treaty under which the saracens restored Bethlehem, Jerusalem and Nazareth to the crusaders, as well granting a secure land corridor for pilgrims linking Jerusalem to the coast, and, finally,

guaranteeing a 10-year respite from hostilities. For his part, Frederick had to make a few token gestures towards the saracens, but they were minor and he undoubtedly got by far the best of the deal and obtained greater benefits for the crusaders than all the fighting of the previous five crusades.

With the way now open, Frederick completed his personal pilgrimage to Jerusalem, where he crowned himself king on February 18, 1229. Despite this achievement, Frederick was still labelled as an excommunicate, and was shunned by both the clergy and the lay leaders of the Latin states. Indeed, the Pope proclaimed a crusade against Frederick himself, declared the emperor's lands in southern Italy forfeit and despatched papal troops, commanded by Frederick's

ABOVE: Having set out for Egypt, King Louis IX of France changed his mind, ordering his ships to head for Tunis instead. He died there, his last word being "Jerusalem".

father-in-law, John of Brienne, to occupy Naples. Hearing of these events, Frederick left the Holy Land, reaching his possessions on Italy in May 1229, where he expelled the papal troops and quickly regained such a strong position that he was able to make made peace with the Pope in August.

THE SEVENTH CRUSADE (1248-1254)

Nearly twenty years passed between Frederick's Sixth Crusade and the next large expedition to the Middle East, which was organised and financed by King Louis IX of France in response to the saracen recapture of Jerusalem in 1244. Louis devoted four years to carefully planning and making elaborate preparations for his ambitious expedition. In fact, the administrative preparations were masterly and worked brilliantly, with sufficient transport and, astonishingly, plenty of money. All this completed, Louis and his army sailed at the end of August 1248, their first destination being the island of Cyprus, where they spent the winter in further preparations.

Louis's strategy was essentially the same as that of the Fifth Crusade and involved a landing in Egypt and establishing a secure base there before marching across the Sinai Desert in order to approach the Holy Land from the south. Louis and his army duly made a very successful landing in Egypt on June 5, 1249, and scored an immediate success by capturing Damietta the following day, something it had taken the Fifth Crusade eighteen months to achieve. But the next phase of the campaign, the attack on Mansurah proved to be quite as catastrophic as that of the Fifth Crusade.

Having advanced, the crusaders found themselves on the opposite bank of a tributary of the Nile to their enemy and were forced to try to construct a causeway across. They were bombarded day and night by barrels containing "Greek Fire", but in February 1250 they found a ford and sent a cavalry force across. However, the knights involved became over-excited by their success and charged into the city of Mansurah, where they were annihilated in the network of narrow, winding streets. Louis also crossed and won the initial encounter with the saracens, but by the end of March the army was suffering so badly from a variety of illnesses, including dysentery and scurvy, that Louis was forced to order a withdrawal, in the course of which he was captured. A huge ransom was demanded for the king and other nobles, which, despite its size, was paid very quickly. Once again Damietta was handed back to the Egyptians and the crusaders sailed away after a humiliating defeat. Most of the army returned to France, but Louis went to Palestine, where he spent four years building fortifications and strengthening the defences of the Latin Kingdom and then, in the spring of 1254, he and his few remaining troops also returned to France.

THE EIGHTH CRUSADE (1270)

King Louis IX also organized the last major crusade in 1270, but by this time the French nobility was distinctly unenthusiastic, and, for reasons which have never been made clear, he decided at the last minute to direct the expedition against the city of Tunis rather than Egypt, as originally planned. However, Tunis was well defended and once again the crusaders were struck down by disease, the whole affair ending abruptly when Louis himself died on August 25, 1270. It was said that his final whispered words were: "Jerusalem, Jerusalem".

THE END OF THE CRUSADES

Throughout these later years the remaining Latin outposts in the Holy Land came under increasingly heavy attack from the saracens who took the crusader cities and castles one by one until the crusader states themselves collapsed. Finally, only one major stronghold, Acre, remained, a city that had been fought over so often. When that, too, fell on May 18, 1291, the final crusader outpost had gone. The remaining crusaders took refuge on Cyprus and later on Rhodes, while some other Latin states, which had been established in Greece during the time of the Fourth Crusade, survived until the mid-15th Century. The fall of Acre signalled the effective end of the crusades, but remnants of these great undertakings have, however, lived on into the 21st Century, as will be described later.

THE POPULAR CRUSADES

LEFT: Peter the Hermit had great success in recruiting for his "People's Crusade". Sadly, it was a total disaster and most died.

BELOW RIGHT: Greatest disaster was the Children's Crusade, which led tens of thousands of innocents to death or slavery.

When Pope Urban II proposed a Crusade to free the Holy Land, it was tacitly assumed that those involved would be nobles or knights, with common people taking part as foot soldiers, retainers or servants, and with the whole under royal, or at least aristocratic, command. Therefore it came as a great surprise when, on various occasions during the period, the crusading message received a strong and vital response from groups of "common people" who decided to organise and participate in their own crusades. It should be noted, however, that despite being named "crusades" these undertakings did not really merit such a title since not only did they not have official (ie, Papal) approval, but all responsible authorities (both lay and clerical) were opposed to them.

THE PEOPLE'S CRUSADE

The first manifestation of this "popular" support came with the "People's Crusade" which was a response to the very first call from Pope Urban II in November 1095. The instigator was a priest, Peter the Hermit, who began preaching his message in Picardy but then travelled around France on a donkey, arousing passionate responses wherever he went. He soon had many followers, including not only many "common people" but also a number of minor nobles and knights. Peter the Hermit reached the city of Cologne in April 1096 where he was joined by a large number of Germans, but from this

point onwards matters began to deteriorate, and the would-be crusaders set out in a number of different parties.

The first group to depart was French, some 2-3,000 strong, who were impatient to get started. Led by a knight named Walter the Penniless, they followed the Danube, passing through Vienna, Belgrade and Sofia until they reached Constantinople, where they stopped until caught up by the group led by Peter the Hermit, with which they then merged.

A second group, possibly some 10,000 strong, was led by a German priest named Volkmar. They reached Prague in May 1096, where, among other things, they terrorised the city's Jewish population. They were totally dispersed by Hungarian troops near the town of Nith. A third group was led by a German priest named Gottschalk, but it too got no further than Hungary before being dispersed by local troops.

The largest group, some 20,000 strong, was led by Peter himself, and this group struggled across Europe, antagonising one community after another, causing destruction and some deaths as they passed through. Despite having many adventures, most of them actually managed to reach the northern shore of the Bosphorus in August 1096. The Byzantine authorities were appalled at the prospect of their city being filled by such people and were so anxious to see them on their way that they provided free shipping to transport the pilgrims across the Bosphorus. At this point Peter's group was joined not only by the group led by Walter the Penniless but also by some Italians, who had arrived separately. By the time they set out on their journey across Anatolia the number had increased to some 25,000, but by now the mass of people was so large and made up of such disparate groups that they were unmanageable and increasingly ill-disciplined. Thus, once in territory controlled by the Seljuk Turks, they could not provide effective resistance to the increasingly frequent attacks until one final massacre near Nicaea (modern Iznik) virtually wiped them out. A few thousand survivors were rescued by the Byzantines and allowed to depart homewards.

THE CHILDREN'S CRUSADE

The Children's Crusade was an emotional and apparently spontaneous movement, forming one of the more astonishing responses to crusading fervour. It began in two separate places in June 1212. In the first, a young shepherd named Stephen, from Cloyes, near Vendôme, France, had a vision in which Jesus commanded him to raise an army to aid the Holy Land.

In view of the general crusader fervour of the times, he had little difficulty in recruiting a band of followers, which included both adults and children, and he then led them to Paris in an effort to persuade the French king, Philip II, to take up the crusade with them. However, the king convinced them to return to their homes and the great majority appear to have done so.

The second, but apparently unrelated, manifestation took place at exactly the same time, but was inspired by a boy named Nicholas from Cologne in Germany, whose followers came mainly from the Rhineland and Lower Lorraine. He assured his recruits that God would help them take Jerusalem back from the saracens and then led them south towards the Mediterranean. As they passed through Mainz some children were persuaded to return home, but the majority pressed on through southern Germany and Austria, and then across the Alps into Italy, where they split up. One group headed for Venice, another headed still further south to Rome, while a third headed westwards and turned up in Marseille in France. The main group, however, wended its way through Piacenza and arrived at the port of Genoa. A few may actually have reached the Holy Land and some may have been taken in by friendly people along the route, but the great majority either were sold into slavery or died.

A very few of these children actually returned to their homes but, as far as the great majority of families were concerned, their children simply walked away one day and disappeared without trace. This was the most tragic of all the episodes in the crusader saga and remains as a pathetic reflection on the religious fervour of the times.

THE SHEPHERD'S CRUSADES

When news of the tragic end of the Seventh Crusade reached western Europe in late 1250 it caused, as such bad news from the Holy Land usually did, a strong reaction, not least among the common people. The most positive manifestation of this came from a group raised by an elderly man known as the "Master of Hungary" who was said to be sixty years old, which, if true, meant that he might have taken part in the Children's Crusade (or at least been aware of it) in his youth.

Whatever the background, he conceived the idea that shepherds had a special role to play in the recovery of the Holy Land, playing on their popular image as simple and honest rustics. He also reminded his audiences of the ideas of Jesus as the "Good Shepherd" and the Paschal Lamb, and one of the most popular banners used by the movement depicted an image of the Cross with a lamb at its foot.

The Master of Hungary began to preach his doctrine in France shortly after Easter in 1251. Following a large rally in the French city of Amiens he led them, now numbering many thousands, to Paris. There, the leaders were received by Queen Blanche, who was serving as regent while her son, Louis IX, was on his crusade, but matters soon turned sour and many

rallies turned into anti-clerical riots, with priests being wounded or, in some cases, killed. The movement gradually disintegrated; a few members reached the Mediterranean coast, but could find no ships. Some, for reasons that are not now apparent, even went northwards to England where they were given a very hostile reception. The more fortunate remainder quietly returned to their villages and their flocks. The idea of a "Shepherd's Crusade" was resurrected in 1321 but after some initial fervour it turned out to be even more short-lived than the first.

COUNT EMICH VON LEININGEN

Count Emich von Leiningen in Swabia (Schwaben) led another "unofficial" crusade in 1096, at the same time as that of Peter the Hermit, but since he was a nobleman his cannot be described as a "people's" crusade. Emich claimed to have woken one morning to find that a crucifix had been miraculously branded onto his chest. He rapidly assembled a group to obey the Pope's call to free the Holy Land. He was imbued with a particularly virulent form of anti-Semitism and he and his followers killed as many Jews as they could find during their journey across Europe, until they were attacked and dispersed in Hungary in the summer of 1096.

Chapter 2

THE MILITARY ORDERS

One of the major phenomena during the crusades was the emergence of the "military orders", members of which epitomised the two medieval ideals of the warrior and religion. Members were sincerely religious people, but they combined those beliefs with a warrior's code and were dedicated to killing their enemies. Some of these orders exerted a major influence and although the crusader orders, such as the Knights Templar, Knights Hospitaller, and the Teutonic Knights, were the better known in Europe, the original order, and one which had a marked influence on the foundation and organisation of the crusader orders, was actually part of the Islamic world.

HASHISHIYYIN (ASSASSINS)

The Islamic military order was known by its Arabic name of hashishiyyin, supposedly because its members carried out their attacks while under the influence of the drug hashish, and they became known throughout Europe as the "Assassins". The original group never numbered more than a few hundred and carried out a relatively small number of killings between about 1090 and 1256, but the majority of their victims were important personages with the result that to this day almost every political murder anywhere in the world is designated an "assassination" and its perpetrator, whatever his or her motive or religious beliefs, is called an "assassin".

In order to understand the Assassins it is necessary to go back to the events following the death of the Prophet Mohammed in 632AD. At that time his followers split into two groups, the largest group being the orthodox Sunnis, who believed that the elected caliphs of Baghdad were the proper leaders. The other, smaller group – the Shias – believed that authority lay with the imams (priests) who were the direct descendants of Mohammed through his daughter Fatimah and his son-in-law Ali, and that one of these would eventually return as the "guided one" – the Mahdi – to establish the rule of justice.

Some one hundred years later, following the death of Ja'afar as-Sadiq, the sixth Imam, in 765, the Shias themselves split into two groups. One believed that Ja'afar's successor was his son Musa and that the Mahdi would be the twelfth in that line, while the other group supported Ja'afar's eldest son, Ismail, and believed the Mahdi would be the seventh in the line. The latter group, known from their leader's name as the Ismailis, became very powerful, establishing the Fatimid caliphate (named after the Prophet's daughter) which ruled Egypt, Sicily and Tunisia from its capital in Cairo, until toppled by the Sunni warrior leader, Saladin, in 1171.

A Persian, Hassan as-Sabah, was born a mainstream Shia in the early part of the 11th Century, but converted to Ismaili in 1072 and became a respected religious teacher. He then decided to set up his own group and sent out teachers, named dias, to win converts. He selected as his base a castle on a rocky pinnacle near the northern Persian city of Daylam in the Elburz Mountains. This virtually impregnable castle was known as Alamut (Eagle's Nest) and Hassan took it from its previous owner by infiltrating his followers a few at a time until he was in a position to take control.

The first Grand Master, Hassan, was an ascetic who spent most of his time in religious contemplation and study, but he also trained a small number of the fittest and most dedicated of his followers as an elite corps of killers, who waged war by carefully staged and skilfully

RIGHT: King Richard I of England, Lionheart, views the city of Jerusalem, the goal of his crusade, which he was fated never to reach. One of the most admired of all English kings, he was also a great commander, showing a firm grasp not only of both strategy and tactics, but also of logistics. Above all, he always led from the front and his personal bravery and concern for his men made him greatly loved by those he commanded.

carried out murders of particular individuals. In this, Hassan's primary targets were other Muslim leaders, his first significant victim being Nizar al-Mulk, the Grand Vizier of Persia, while another was the Prince of Emessa, who was murdered while en route to attack the invading crusaders in 1102. These killings were not seen as random acts of murder, but as carefully controlled and executed religious acts, whose sanctity was ensured because the dagger used in the deed had always been blessed by the Grand Master for the murder of a specific individual.

Because their modus operandi was to despatch their victims by a blow from a dagger at very close quarters, the Assassins were, of necessity, particularly adept at disguising themselves. Thus, they learnt to blend in so well that they could get close to their intended targets – most of whom were important and well-protected people – without arousing any suspicion. One important aspect of these assassinations was that time was not a factor; thus, there was no question of hurry and some attacks took years to achieve.

Hassan was a great expert at what today would be termed "psychological warfare". On several occasions leaders woke to find an unsheathed dagger laid nearby, making it clear that they could have been killed had that been Hassan's intention. Also, the actual killings caused a reign of fear, with rulers becoming suspicious of even their most loyal courtiers. Saladin, who was a brave man by any standard, knew that he was a target and took to avoiding all contact with strangers and to sleeping in a wooden tower.

Hassan demanded the most absolute loyalty from his followers and was, himself, utterly ruthless. He demonstrated this on several occasions by ordering followers to commit immediate suicide to demonstrate their loyalty. He also ordered the deaths of several of his sons – one for breaking the rule that banned drinking alcohol, another because he plotted the death of another assassin.

Hassan as-Sabah died in 1124 and his policies were continued more or less unchanged by the next two leaders of his group. Under these men a second Persian Grand Vizier was murdered in his own stables in 1127, the Fatimid caliph was murdered in Cairo in 1130, and the Caliph of Baghdad in 1139. All three victims were very important people and aware of their danger, but despite the protection of numerous guards they were unable to avoid the assassin's dagger.

The fourth Grand Master, Hassan II, took office in 1162 and then tried to convert the Assassin beliefs into a new and separate religion, independent of Islam. But this was too much for his followers and he became their victim, being murdered by his brother-in-law in 1166. The movement returned to their Islamic beliefs, while still maintaining the independence established by their original Grand Master, but, mainly through the influences of geography and distance, had split into two semi-autonomous wings. One of these, the Persian wing, was still based in the original stronghold of Alamut.

The second group, which became far more closely involved with the crusaders, was located in Syria, being based in the mountains south of Antioch at the castle of Kahf, which the Assassins had bought from the local emir in 1135. This Syrian wing was led from 1162 to 1192 by Sinan ibn Salman ibn Mohammed and allegedly turned to killing for money rather than for purely religious reasons. Sinan exercised a rule of terror from his stronghold and became known to the crusaders as "the Old Man of the Mountains".

Despite the depredations of the crusaders, the Assassins still concentrated most of their efforts on fellow Muslims and Sinan twice sent men to kill Saladin, but they failed and Saladin responded by raiding Ismaili territory. According to many reports, Saladin was persuaded to desist when, despite the most stringent safety precautions, he woke one morning to find a poisoned dagger lying on his pillow next to his head, placed there as a warning.

The first known crusader victim of the Assassins was Count Raymond II of Tripoli who was murdered in 1152. Raymond's mother-in-law, Queen Melisende, and his wife, Countess Hodierna, were setting out from Tripoli to Jerusalem and Raymond escorted them for a short distance at the start of their journey. Then, his duty done, he rode back to Tripoli accompanied by a small escort. As he rode through the city gate he was suddenly attacked by a group of Assassins, who killed him and two of his escorts, and then disappeared, never to be caught.

Then in 1192 two Assassins disguised themselves as Christian converts to kill another

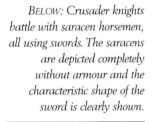

BELOW: Crusader knights battle with saracen horsemen, all using swords. The saracens are depicted completely without armour and the characteristic shape of the sword is clearly shown.

target, Conrad of Montferrat, who had just been selected as the next King of Jerusalem and was about to go to the Holy City to claim his crown. One evening Conrad was walking in the street of the city he ruled, Tyre, when, rounding a corner, he was confronted by two men, one of whom appeared to hold out a letter. Conrad reached out to accept it and as he did so the second man killed him with a single blow of a dagger. One of the killers was despatched on the spot, but the other was caught and tortured before being killed. It was established that the two men were followers of the "Old Man of the Mountains" but a malicious rumour was put about suggesting that they had been paid by Richard Coeur de Lion, although whether this was true or not and what he might have gained from it were never established.

Obviously, when on an operation the Assassin elite wore nothing that would associate them with their order. However, when inside their strongholds the Assassin rafiqs wore white tunics, with red caps and belts, signifying a mixture of innocence and blood.

Even the Assassins' day passed, however. In the mid-13th Century the Mongols penetrated former Islamic territories from the east, and Hulagu, grandson of the great Genghis Khan, took the Persian strongholds one by one, razing them to the ground and massacring their garrisons as he did so. Finally, even the fortress of Alamut was destroyed in 1256. In Syria, the other major branch of the Assassins was overcome by the Sultan Al-Zahir Beybars in campaigns in the 1260s and 1270s.

Tiny in numbers, the Assassins caused fear and dread among the contemporary rulers of Europe and the Middle East, and for many decades any attempt on the life of a leader was, at least initially, blamed on them. Not only that, however, but their name and their method of operation has remained in use in both the English and French languages from that day to this.

THE CHRISTIAN ORDERS

The authentic Christian military orders had three essential elements. The order had to be recognised by the Pope, and the swords had to be worn by authority of the prince. Members were thus recognised by both Church and State, but in addition they had to vow to follow a very specific code of discipline which bound them together as members of a close-knit confraternity. The original military orders were founded in the Holy Land but others were later founded to serve in Spain, Portugal, and in the Baltic provinces.

LEFT: King Richard I of
England. The second son of
King Henry II and Queen
Eleanor of Aquitaine (see
pages 32-33), he was his
mother's favourite son, and
she was his regent in England
during his absence on the
crusade. After all his great
adventures in so many battles
his death came about in a
very minor engagement in
France in 1199, when he was
wounded by an arrow and
the wound festered.

As far as the crusades were concerned there were two main orders – the Knights Templar and the Knights Hospitaller – and several minor orders, of which the Teutonic Order was the most significant, and these are described below. The general concept of the military orders also resulted in numbers of similar orders in other parts of Europe, mainly concerned with the fighting in the Iberian peninsula and in the Baltic territories, and these are also mentioned, for completeness.

The orders were generally similar with a very rigid hierarchy, headed by a Grand Master. The military brethren of the orders were divided into two classes: knights, who were never very numerous, who were the *corps d'elite* and formed the heavy cavalry; and the men-at-arms (sergeants) who were, in effect, the light cavalry. For infantry and the many administrative duties that are part of any campaign, the orders also employed large numbers of mercenaries, many of whom were enlisted in the Holy Land itself, and these were known as turcopoles. These men were not, of course, members of the order for which they were fighting.

There were also two categories of non-combatant members of the orders. One was the chaplains, who performed the religious functions and duties both in the abbeys and on campaign. The other category was the casaliers, who were responsible for the day-to-day administration of the order and its property.

KNIGHTS TEMPLAR

After the First Crusade had culminated in taking Jerusalem in 1099 most crusaders considered that their duty had been done and returned home, leaving only a relatively small number – perhaps as few as five hundred – in the Holy Land. Such a small number needed to be concentrated to be militarily effective, but there was also a need for many more knights to be spread across the major routes for the maintenance of control and to protect and escort the pilgrims. This latter requirement led to the founding of small groups of knights, the first of which was formed in 1115. This group initially comprised just two Burgundian knights, Hugues des Payens and Godfroi de St Omer, who could afford only one horse between them, and was titled the "Order of the Poor Knights of Christ", with poverty being part of their vow. Impressed by their work, King Baldwin of Jerusalem gave them accommodation in a building on the supposed site of Solomon's Temple, which led to them being given the popular name

RIGHT: A scene in one of the
great castles, where a pilgrim
(seated) describes his
experiences to knights of the
two great military orders. In
the centre is a Knight
Hospitaller in a black cloak,
and next to him a Knight
Templar in his white cloak.

of Knights of the Temple of Solomon, or "Knights Templar", for short.

The group increased in reputation and numbers and in 1124 it became an official order of warrior-monks, with rules based on those of the Cistercian Order and drafted in part by St. Bernard of Clairveaux. For convenience, the vows can be divided into two principal elements. The first were military and included fighting to the death for the Holy Places; refusing to be ransomed if captured; accepting any combat, regardless of the odds; defending any Christian molested by Muslims; and refusing quarter or ransom to Muslims. The second part of the vows focused essentially on monastic matters and included forswearing purchasing entry into the Order, murder, treason, desertion, heresy, plotting, disobedience, consorting with women, and trying to escape from the Order. They also swore to preserve the secrets of the Order.

There is some evidence that Hugues de Payens based the organisation of his new Order upon that of the Assassins. Thus, the hierarchy of Grand Master, Seneschal, Deputy Master, Marshal, and Masters of Provinces was virtually identical to that used by the Assassins, as was the geographical split into provinces, each of which was sub-divided into preceptories (houses), each under a commander.

The dominant members of the Order were the knights, who alone were allowed to wear the distinctive dress of the order, a large white mantle with a small red Latin cross on the left chest and a much larger cross on the back. Each of these knights was allowed three horses, plus a squire mounted on fourth horse, but, in accordance with the vows of poverty, everything else belonged to the Order. There was also a subordinate class of member, designated sergeants-at-arms. The ranks of the knights were increased from two sources: one was a group known as "confrère knights" who served on limited engagements, sometimes as long as several years; the other source was knights who lived on properties owned by the Order and who therefore owed it military service. Chaplains made up the other class of full member.

Having been endorsed by the Pope, the Order rapidly became very wealthy, receiving many gifts of both money and property. As it prospered, the Order established preceptories throughout Europe which were responsible, within their designated area, for representing the interests of the Order, recruiting new members, and administering the lands and estates now owned by the Templars.

The Templars quickly became a military force to be reckoned with, since their tight-knit organisation, iron discipline and ruthlessness gained them a high reputation among Christians and Muslims alike. In battle they always took position of honour on right of the line, but one consequence of their vows was that the death rate was particularly high, and between its foundation and leaving the Holy Land the order lost some 20,000 knights and sergeants.

The headquarters was located at Jerusalem until the city fell in 1187, when it was transferred in turn to Antioch, Acre, Caeserea, and finally to Cyprus.

Having started to raise money in Europe, the Templars soon found themselves regularly transferring their own funds and supplies to the Holy Land, which forced them to set up an efficient banking and transfer system. Seeing the Templars' capabilities, rulers, the nobility and individuals soon started to use it as well. Crusaders found it particularly convenient to deposit money at their local preceptory and then carry letters of credit that could be encashed at any Templar preceptory along the route. As a result, the Templars quickly became bankers for much of Europe, and also extremely wealthy, and their business interests expanded into money-lending as well as providing ships in the Mediterranean to carry pilgrims direct to and from the Holy Land.

Having been forced out of the Holy Land at the end of the crusading period, the Templars moved to Cyprus where the Order had no real military role, so it concentrated on its banking and money-lending businesses. As a result, its power and influence were soon being regarded with enmity and jealousy, and eventually led to its downfall when, in 1307, King Philip of France (with the connivance of Pope Clement V) arrested all but a very few members of the Order in his country. These leading Templars were tortured and eventually forced to "confess" to such sins as Satanism, homosexuality, blasphemy and corruption, and the great majority were subsequently burnt at the stake. The Order was officially suppressed in 1312 by Pope Clement V and most of its property was seized by Philip in France and Edward II in England.

THE HOSPITALLERS OF ST. JOHN OF JERUSALEM

The second of the great knightly orders was known as the Hospitallers of Jerusalem from the movement's foundation in about 1113 until 1309, when they became known as the Knights of Rhodes. That name continued until 1522 when it changed to the Knights of Malta and has remained unchanged since then, but it is as the Hospitallers that they will be described here.

The movement had its origins in a hospice (from the Latin hospitia) named after St. John the Baptist, which was founded in Jerusalem at the beginning of the 12th Century and run by a Brother Gerard, following the rules of the Augustine order. The care of the sick rendered by Gerard and his fellow brothers so impressed Godfrey of Bouillon that he made them a grant of land in Jerusalem to help them with their work. As with the Templars, this generous gift was followed by many others, and the Order quickly accumulated land and revenues in Sicily, Italy and Provence. Indeed, by the time that Gerard died in 1120 the Hospitallers had been recognised as an independent Order by the Pope and was very wealthy, having established a series of hospices and hospitals throughout the Holy Land.

The Order of St. John was entitled by its Papal charter to defend its hospitals, Jerusalem and its own people, and this led to the setting up of a military arm. A sub-group was also formed – the Canons of the Holy Sepulchre – made up of knights who guarded the tomb of Christ. These wore a white surcoat with a single red cross on it. In the field each knight was allowed his own four horses and two esquires, while a sergeant had two horses and, from 1302, one esquire.

ABOVE: A Knight of the Order of the Hospitallers of St. John of Jerusalem, painted by Titian. The Order has continued in existence down to the present day, but has long since abandoned its military activities, now concentrating on charitable work.

RIGHT: A Knight Hospitaller (top); a foot soldier of the Order (bottom right); and a turcopole, a Syrian mercenary (bottom left). All are from the 12th-13th Century period.

As the Order gained in wealth, power and numbers its influence and responsibilities also grew. It was given the castle of Gibelin in 1136, two more castles in 1139 and four more in 1142, the latter including Krak des Chevaliers. The problem with such castles was that, despite (or, perhaps, because of) their strength and imposing appearance, they required adequate garrisons for proper defence, which even the Hospitallers did not have. Thus, all that the Order could spare for the finest of them all, the Krak des Chevaliers, were 200 knights and sergeants, whereas the previous garrison had numbered 2,000.

At the head of the Order was the Grand Commander and below him the Order was divided into two arms, the hospitallers – brothers and sisters – and the military arm, made up of knights, sergeants and confrères. The Grand Commander was located in the Holy Land and was supported by a number of officials, including the marshal (who was head of the military arm), the hospitaller, the treasurer, the drapier (quartermaster), and the turcopolier, who commanded and administered the turcopoles (locally enlisted light cavalry).

In Europe there were seven "langues" (tongues), each of which was divided into "priories" (provinces), run by a prior, and these, in their turn, were divided into a number of "commanderies", run by commanders. Such commanders' responsibilities included collecting the revenues from the Order's properties in his area and, having made an agreed deduction

for the running of his own commandery, sending all the rest, known as the responsion, to the Holy Land for the maintenance of the Order there.

One of the great scandals of the crusades was that in the 13th Century the Templars and the Hospitallers fell out with each other. Thus, despite having common goals in protecting Christian interests in the Holy Land and in "killing the infidel", they actually devoted much of their considerable energy to fighting each other, disputing possession of various cities. By the middle of the 13th Century they were actually killing each other in the streets of Acre.

But Jerusalem was lost in 1243, Gaza in 1244 (where no fewer than three hundred Hospitallers were captured), and in 1271 they even lost the Krak des Chevaliers. Tripoli fell in 1289 and the final foothold, Acre, in 1291, where every single Hospitaller died.

The remnants of the Hospitallers then moved to a new base in Cyprus, where they quickly assumed a naval role and soon had their own fleet of galleys and galleases. This led to their attack on saracen-occupied Rhodes, which lasted, from 1306 to 1309 and, when successful, the Order transferred its base to Rhodes from where it soon asserted naval domination over the eastern Mediterranean. The Hospitallers' stay in Rhodes lasted for just over two centuries, but in 1522 they were expelled by the Turks and moved again, this time to Malta.

Like the Templars, the Hospitallers were granted extensive rights and privileges by the Pope. They enjoyed absolute independence of all spiritual and temporal authority save that of Rome, exemptions from tithes (parish land taxes imposed by the Church), and had the right to maintain their own chapels, clergy and cemeteries. Both Orders were charged with the defence of the Holy Land and between the two of them they owned virtually all the castles in the Holy Land, the Hospitallers having seven and the Templars the remainder. The Hospitallers had the benefit of the income of some 140 estates in the Holy Land, and during the 13th Century they were said to own more than 13,000 manses and manors in Europe

The Hospitallers followed the rules of the Augustinian and Benedictine monks, so, like them, they wore a black mantle with an in-built cowl. Their symbol as crusaders was a white cross worn on the chest of the mantle, and the same type of cross was worn on the left shoulder of the black cloak. The shields were painted an overall black with a white cross.

THE ORDER OF TEUTONIC KNIGHTS

A Teutonic hospital was established in Jerusalem in the early 12th Century, under the jurisdiction of the Grand Master of the Order of St. John (the "Hospitallers"), but it was expelled with other crusaders when Saladin took the city in 1187. Then in 1190, during the Third Crusade's siege of Acre, a new temporary Teutonic hospital was set up in the crusaders' camp outside the walls of Acre. Resources were scarce, so ships' sails and spars were used to create a large tent where wounded German crusaders could be cared for. Then, when the siege was successfully completed and the saracen garrison surrendered, the hospital was moved into the city where it became permanent.

Within a few years the Teutonic Order had gathered strength, with branches in various countries, and in 1196 it was recognised by Pope Celestine III. In 1197 a meeting was held in Jerusalem, where it was decided that in their military activities members would follow the Rule of the Templars, while in caring for the poor and sick they would follow the Rule of St. John's Hospital in Jerusalem. It then received full, formal recognition from Pope Innocent III in 1199 and in 1205 he granted members the right to wear a white habit with a black cross.

The Order was headed by a Grand Master (Hochmeister), the first being Hermann von Salza. Like the Templars and Hospitallers, the new Order was given many gifts and became prosperous. In the Holy Land, however, the Teutonic Order was always the poor relation to the Templars and Hospitallers, who had already bought most of the available land and castles.

The Hospitallers and Templars were always international in their appeal and membership, but the Teutonic Knights had clear ties with Germany from the very start. This, combined with the Order's inability to expand its lands and influence in the Holy Land, led to its early departure from the Middle East. Even when Frederick II was proclaimed King of Jerusalem in 1229 and the Teutonic Knights provided the guard of honour at his coronation, they could not break into the magic circle and so the Order began to concentrate its activities on extending Germanic control and influence along the Baltic littoral. The Order's headquarters remained in Acre until 1291 when it moved to Venice, but it stayed there only until 1309, when the Hochmeister moved it to Marienburg in East Prussia.

OTHER MILITARY ORDERS

There were a number of other, much smaller military orders, all of which were founded on similar basic principles to those established by the Templars and Hospitallers. Three of them were directly associated with the crusades in the Holy Land. The others, however, confined their activities to the Iberian peninsula, Italy or the Prussian Baltic provinces, but are mentioned briefly here because of the similarities to their more famous brothers.

HOLY LAND
THE KNIGHTS OF ST. LAZARUS

One of the scourges of the era was leprosy and the Order of St. Lazarus was founded in Jerusalem early in the 12th Century specifically for those suffering from the disease. By about 1130 the Order was running a leper hospital in Jerusalem and by 1150 there were further hospitals at various other sites in the Holy Land. The Order started a small military wing, consisting of knights and sergeants, who took part in various campaigns and sieges, and all members who fought at the siege of Acre in 1291 perished. The Order then moved to Cyprus and later to France where it ceased to exist in the late 18th Century. Any Templar or Hospitaller who developed leprosy had no choice but to transfer to this Order.

HOSPITALLERS OF ST. THOMAS OF CANTERBURY

This was the only specifically English order and was founded in about 1190 to help nurse the sick, particularly the English, at the siege of Acre. There was a small military arm, known as the Knights of St. Thomas Acon, who, like so many others, perished to the last man at the fall of Acre in 1291. Their distinguishing mark was a cross, divided vertically into red and white segments. Although well funded, the Order was always small in number, most English knights preferring to join the Hospitallers.

LEFT: The tomb of a Knight Hospitaller, who was buried on Rhodes, an island ruled by the Order from 1309 to 1522. The tomb has since been moved to Istanbul, where it now rests.

KNIGHTS OF OUR LADY OF MOUNTJOIE

Founded in about 1175 in the Holy Land and recognised by the Pope in 1180, this military order was essentially Spanish, although membership was open to any nationality. It main base in the Holy Land was Mountjoie castle, which was located just outside Jerusalem. Most of its members perished at the Battle of Hattin, following which most of the remainder joined the Templars, while the others returned to Spain where they were absorbed into the Knights of Calatrava in 1221.

SPAIN

Both the Hospitallers and the Templars had recruiting bases in Spain, but did not take part in the campaigns there. This led to the founding of a number of military orders, whose specific role was confined to the fighting in the Iberian peninsula.

KNIGHTS OF CALATRAVA

Founded in about 1160, specifically for the defence of Calatrava, a royal fortress, the Order became very powerful in the 13th Century, but then declined and had ceased to exist by about 1500.

KNIGHTS OF ST. IAGO

Founded in about 1160, the Knights of St. Iago (Saint James) were originally tasked to protect pilgrims on their journeys to and from the shrine at St. Iago at Compostella. The Order expanded and was granted a Papal charter in 1175, which established that it would follow the rule of St. Augustin in most respects. Unlike Augustinians, however, the Knights of St. Iago were allowed to own property and to marry.

RIGHT: The Teutonic Order: (top), a knight, ca. 1230; (right) sergeant (foot soldier) ca. 1230; and (bottom) a knight ca. 1300. Note the latter's elaborate helmet, designed to impress in battle.

ORDER OF OUR LADY OF RANSOM (NUESTRA SEÑORA DE MERCED)

This group, also known as the "Mercedarians", was a small military order founded in 1218, whose main purpose was to rescue Christians, particularly knights and priests, who had been enslaved by the saracens. In 1317 it was decided that the Grand Master should be a priest as opposed to a knight, as a result of which most of the knight members left, many of them joining the Order of Montesa (*qv*).

KNIGHTS OF ST. GEORGE OF ALFAMA

This Order had a somewhat shadowy existence from about 1200 until 1400 when it was absorbed into the Montesa Order (*qv*).

KNIGHTS OF OUR LADY OF MONTESA

Yet another small Spanish order, this was raised, at least in part, as a response to the disbandment of the Templars. It absorbed, first, a number of knights from the Order of Calatrava and later the remaining members of the Order of St. George of Alfama. Despite these injections of new members it gradually decreased in size and by about 1600 had ceased to exist.

PORTUGAL

KNIGHTS OF CHRIST

This Order was raised in 1312 to counter the power of the Hospitallers and continued until the early 16th Century. Its activities were almost exclusively concerned with exploration and colonisation.

ORDER OF EVORA

This was a very small Portuguese order raised in about 1160, and which for some years was based at Evora, south of Lisbon. Low membership forced the Order to hand over Evora to the Templars and to become part of the Order of Calatrava, although it appears to have retained its name.

RIGHT: The Hofmeister (Grand Master) of the Teutonic Order (left) and a Schwertbrüder, a knight of the "Brethren of the Sword", an order raised to defend the city of Riga.

BELOW: Despite all the battle losses, sickness was the greatest killer during the crusades, as illustrated in this scene from the camp of King Louis IX during the Seventh Crusade, 1248-1254.

HILDIBRAND

ORDER OF AVIZ

Some years later the Order of Evora, still under the jurisdiction of the Calatravans, was given responsibility for the defence of Aviz and it changed its name to the Order of Aviz. Then in 1218 the Order of Calatrava gave up its operations in Portugal, which were passed to the Order of Aviz, and this continued to exist as an independent order well into the 15th Century.

ITALY

ORDER OF ST. JAMES OF ALTOPASCIO

This Order is believed to have been operating in the 10th Century, when it ran a hospital for pilgrims, although its charter as a military order was not approved until 1239. Although it eventually operated hospitals in England, France and Italy, it does not appear to have extended its work to the Holy Land.

GERMANY

BRETHREN OF THE SWORD

The main Germanic order, the Teutonic Order, has already been described. There was, however, one smaller order, which was founded in 1197, specifically for the defence of the city of Riga in Estonia. The full title was Military Brothers of Christ, but its badge of a sword led to members being known as "Brethren of the Sword" (Schwertzbrüder). The Order was later absorbed into the Teutonic Order.

THE CONTRIBUTION OF THE ORDERS

From the crusaders' point of view the military orders made a major contribution to the various campaigns in the Holy Land. They were well organised and their internal discipline was tight, to say the least. For the saracens the military orders were a fearsome enemy from whom they knew they could expect no quarter and, in consequence, to whom no quarter was given. The military orders were also remarkably independent, owing allegiance to nobody but the Pope, placing them almost totally outside the usual hierarchy of cardinals, bishops and clerics who exerted such tight control over everyday life in medieval Europe.

The members of the orders were bound to follow the monastic way of life, which included reciting the Hours, fasting, penance and celibacy. This did not, however, prevent them from acquiring vast territorial possessions: at the height of their importance the Hospitallers controlled some 13,000 manorial properties throughout Europe, and the Templars a further 9,000. Unlike those of the non-military monastic orders, however, these properties were not independent, but under tight control and required to remit a large proportion of their income to their orders' central funds. The orders also had a highly developed system for transferring those funds to the Holy Land, and then introduced an equally effective system for transferring funds on behalf of others, thus contributing yet further to their wealth.

The trouble was that the orders became too powerful, their wealth, independence and discipline giving them great advantages over virtually anyone else involved in the crusades. Indeed, on several occasions this power enabled one or other of the orders to act as "king makers" in the complicated mechanics of selecting a King of Jerusalem. Such power led to considerable arrogance, with the top officials such as the Grand Masters acting in a particularly high-handed manner on occasions. This, in its turn, provoked antagonism, envy and, in the end, hatred. This arrogance also led to bitter feuds between the two orders and at some stages, particularly in the latter days in the Holy Land, Hospitallers and Templars were devoting more energy to murdering each other than to prosecuting the aims of the crusades.

Chapter 3

FORTIFICATIONS AND SIEGE WARFARE

Siege warfare – both conducting sieges and resisting them – was a very important part of all campaigns during the crusades. Castles and the conduct of siege warfare were by no means unknown in early medieval Europe, but when the crusaders reached the Middle East they quickly found that the design of castles and the techniques of attacking them were far more advanced there, and they had to learn rapidly.

Castles were, by definition, built at sites of strategic importance. In peacetime their possession enabled the holder to impose control over the surrounding area and its population, as well as people passing through, and, in particular, to levy taxes. Thus, they were almost invariably built at sites where they dominated important roads, caravan routes, river crossings, mountain passes or frontier crossings. In war, no advancing force could afford to leave an undefeated castle in its rear, since it would then inevitably serve as a base for raids on its lines-of-communication. This led to many spectacular castles being built – the military wonders of their age – and there were some noteworthy sieges during the various crusader campaigns, while the tactics of conducting and resisting sieges became one of the most sophisticated aspects of contemporary warfare.

CASTLES

The aim of the builders of castles was to design an impregnable fortress which, by a combination of design features, would resist any attempt by an attacker to capture it. Such attacks, they knew, would involve either compelling the garrison to capitulate through diplomacy or starvation, or by forcible entry over, through or under the walls.

Crusader castle builders tried, wherever possible, to take advantage of natural features such as rocky outcrops or promontories and, while a few were built on virgin sites, many were developed from earlier Muslim castles, which were either modified or totally rebuilt. The crusaders built a large number of castles throughout the territories they controlled, many of which were eventually owned and run by one or other of the military orders. Indeed, the castle-building programme eventually became over-ambitious and the vast network of castles was eventually impossible to garrison properly, becoming one of the major factors in the crusaders' eventual downfall.

Stone was the preferred building material, since it was resistant to attack, was fireproof, and enabled very large and sophisticated structures to be built. These structures were frequently built on rocky outcrops, some of them both high and with difficult access. Although few details survive, the preparation of the site, the delivery of the materials to the site and the construction process must have been very major – and extremely expensive – undertakings.

Most castles constructed during the crusades consisted of an inner citadel, in itself extremely strong, which was surrounded by an outer wall, thus giving the attacker two quite separate obstacles to penetrate. In addition, if the attackers penetrated the outer wall they frequently found themselves operating in an open area between that and the citadel, where they were extremely vulnerable – what would, in 21st Century terms, be described as a "killing ground".

Both inner and outer walls were interspersed with towers, whose role was two-fold. First, they served as buttresses, thus adding physical strength to the structure. Second, by jutting out from the walls, they also provided positions from which archers could fire into the flanks of assault parties trying to scale the walls. Square towers were easier to construct but it was

RIGHT: The full horror of medieval siege warfare, with a trebuchet launching "Greek Fire" at the castle. The composition of "Greek Fire" is an enduring and still unsolved mystery.

discovered that their corners gave sappers an ideal start point for their demolition work, so hemispherical towers, although more difficult to build, came into fashion.

The tops of walls and towers were lined with battlements with embrasures through which archers could fire or soldiers could drop various unpleasant substances onto the heads of those below. Walls also included "loops" or "loopholes", which were vertical or cruciform slots through which archers could fire without exposing themselves.

The outer wall was frequently surrounded by a deep ditch which in Europe could be flooded to become a moat, although in the Middle East there was seldom sufficient water. It was also important that the area beyond the ditch should be clear to deny attackers protection from both observation and from arrows and other weapons fired from within the castle.

Castle garrisons often included various types of weaponry such as catapults, ballistas and trebuchets. Some were small and mounted on platforms atop towers, but others were large and fired from inside. Some of these were quite accurate and could be used to destroy enemy trebuchets and siege towers, as happened during the siege of Acre.

Obviously, there had to be a means of access to the castle, which required a gate, but this automatically became one of the most vulnerable places in all the defences. Means of improving its security included an extremely robust door, a moat or ditch crossed by a drawbridge that could be raised and lowered, and a portcullis, which was a heavy metal screen which could be raised and lowered to provide the door with additional protection. The crusaders went to even greater lengths to make the entrances to their castles more secure, one means being a right-angled bend immediately inside the gate and a long tunnel containing additional portcullises and loopholes through which arrows could be fired.

Logistical aspects of castle warfare were of great importance. It was well known that one of the first actions of a besieging force would be to close off all movement into and out of the castle, so the castellan had to be prepared for a long period without resupply. He would have a considerable garrison to support, which was usually increased by local peasants and their livestock, who also wanted shelter from the attacker. He would also have horses for the knights

ABOVE: Medieval castles were carefully designed to provide the maximum resistance to an attacker. Note in this one, for example, a reconstruction of the crusader castle at Sendshirli in Syria, how penetrating the main gate (bottom of the picture) only allowed the attackers into an enclosed yard in what would be termed today a "killing ground". Even when they had fought their way through the next wall, the attackers were faced with yet higher walls protecting the keep.

LEFT: *When the men of the First Crusade were preparing for their final assault on Jerusalem in 1099 they made a solemn procession around the walls, led by the bishops carrying the cross, while the saracen defenders watched from the walls and shouted their defiance.*

opportunity to surrender. If the defenders considered their position hopeless they could accept "with honour" and would then normally be allowed to depart peacefully, carrying their arms. But, if they refused and the attackers subsequently carried the fortress by assault, then it was accepted that the latter would "have the right" to sack and pillage, and to execute the defending troops. Even then, however, it was not unknown for victorious commanders to give mercy under certain circumstances.

If diplomacy failed, the next option for the besiegers was to starve the garrison into submission by isolating it and cutting it off from all contact with the outside world. For the attacker this was the most economical course in terms of conserving his men's lives, but it required the besieging army to establish a large camp, which needed to be protected both from forays by the besieged garrison and from an advancing relief force. Such a "siege-by-starvation" could prove very time-consuming, as well as being expensive in terms of supplies, particularly of food, water and fodder, and pay.

Finally, if all else had failed, the only option was to carry out an assault on the stronghold, which required the attacking force to enter the castle through a breach, over the top of the walls or by mining underneath them. Whichever was tried, it was inevitably costly in lives of the attackers (as well as the defenders).

MACHINES

There were a large number of machines associated with siege warfare. These used some iron or steel parts, but the basic construction material was wood, which meant that two of the essentials were a supply of large baulks of timber and a means of transporting them to the scene of the action.

SIEGE TOWER

Known as a belfry (*beffroi*), the siege tower was a very large and costly structure, as well as being, for its time, a complicated piece of engineering, which had to meet a number of "operational requirements". Obviously, it had to be tall enough to exceed the height of the castle wall being attacked, as a result of which some were 100ft (30m) high. It also had to be sufficiently strong and rigid to bear its own weight and that of the knights and other forces

BELOW: *Attacking a fortress was the highest form of medieval warfare and involved a wide range of weapons and a variety of methods of attack and access, all intended to weaken the defenders' resistance as rapidly as possible.*

who would carry out the attack. It could not be constructed in situ since the tower builders would have been under fire from the defenders, so it had to be assembled at a safe distance from the walls, and made sufficiently mobile and stable so that it could be moved into position. Then it needed to incorporate protection for the people inside and to have a drawbridge at the top level which could be lowered onto the castle walls, thus enabling the attackers to cross.

To achieve this the siege tower consisted of several floors (solaria), connected by ladders, with additional cross-braces to give the strength and rigidity required. The front and side walls were covered by timber, often reinforced by iron plates, to provide additional protection and to disguise what was going on from the defenders. This timber facing was often covered by animal hides soaked in vinegar to try to prevent the timbers from catching fire.

Once the tower had been built, any ditch had to be filled in and a fairly level track cleared to get the device to the walls. Nor was one such tower normally sufficient and it was usual for a number to be built to avoid the defenders being able to concentrate their efforts.

The end result was a very substantial piece of engineering. At the siege of Acre in 1188-1191, for example, three towers were built, each of which was some 100ft (30m) high and had five floors. Each tower took many weeks to construct.

Most castle walls were surrounded by a man-made ditch, which had to be filled in to enable the tower to get close enough. Filling in was done by workers protected by mobile screens and roofs, using dirt, earth, stones, rocks, wood and fascines. The resulting pile was then covered with planks to enable the tower to be moved over it. When this had been completed the belfry was moved into position close to the castle wall, by moving it on built-in wheels or rolling it across logs, the motive power being provided by a combination of men inside the tower pushing, and men or oxen pulling on blocks and pulleys. All of this work close to the wall had, of course, to be done under observation and fire of the defenders.

ABOVE: The wooden tower was an essential element of siege warfare. It had to be constructed out of range of the defenders' weapons and then moved into position.

BATTERING RAMS

Battering rams were normally used against the gates of castles, but were sometimes also used against walls. The device consisted of a huge tree trunk that was suspended horizontally from a wooden beam and swung so that its iron-capped end hit the target. The great ram constructed at Acre in 1190, for example, used the mast of a ship. Obviously, the greater the mass of the trunk and the greater its momentum when it hit the target, the more effective it was. Sometimes crews of up to sixty men were used. Protection was required, and this consisted of a sloped roof, which, in the larger machines, was made of wooden slats, covered with metal plates and animal skins soaked in vinegar.

THE BORE

The bore was a large, slow-moving, iron-tipped, horizontally mounted wooden beam, which was slowly rotated so that it drilled a hole into the castle wall. Again, the crew had to be protected by a sloping roof. It is not clear from the records how effective such a machine might have been, much depending, presumably, on the effectiveness of the iron head, the rate of rotation and the pressure with which it was brought to bear.

THE MANGON AND TREBUCHET

The mangon and trebuchet were the direct precursors of artillery, being used to project a payload – usually, stones or a rock – over a distance. Both worked on the principle of the lever, with a long wooden beam pivoted asymmetrically between two uprights, and operated by bringing the shorter arm smartly downwards, thus launching the payload, which was at the end of the longer arm, either in a cup or a sling. This beam (or possibly several beams lashed together) was probably a maximum of 30ft (9m) long.

BELOW: Battering rams were made from a tree trunk and usually given an iron tip. The operators were a natural target for the defenders and had to be protected.

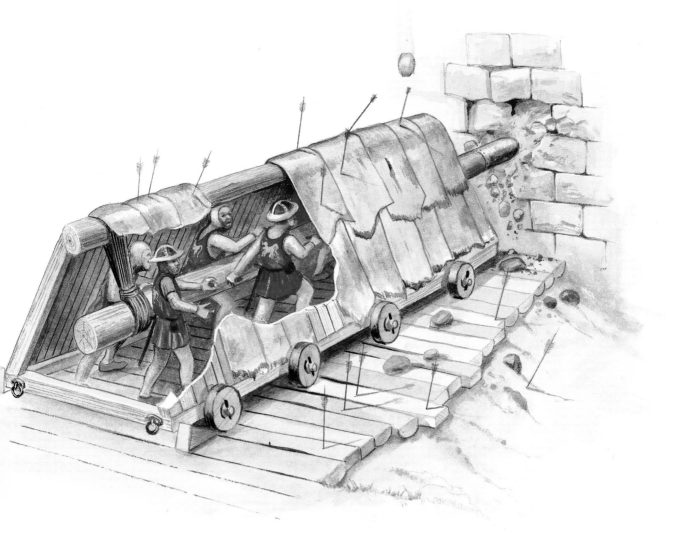

The earlier type, which dated back to Roman times, was the mangon (or its smaller version, the mangonel), which employed a system in which the beam was mounted in several skeins of twisted rope. When pulled back by a winch or pulleys the skeins were placed in torsion, and when these were released the beam was rotated until it hit a padded wooden beam, causing the projectile to be launched on its trajectory.

The other system was known in the West as the trebuchet and appears to have been invented by the Arabs, probably in the 8th or 9th Centuries AD. This machine also employed a beam, but in this case the shorter arm was moved either by men pulling on ropes (the "traction trebuchet") or by a container loaded with rocks, stones, or earth (the "counterweight trebuchet"). At the end of the longer arm was the payload, sometimes carried in a cup, but more usually in a sling. The size and nature of the payload depended upon the design of the machine but normally consisted of rocks. Maintaining a supply of rocks would have represented a significant and manpower-intensive logistic problem. Other payloads are reported to have included dead soldiers' heads or bodies and rotting animal carcasses, intended to spread disease – early forms of psychological and bacteriological warfare. Also, on at least one occasion, an unfortunate live messenger was returned to his castle by means of the trebuchet.

The actual performance of these machines is difficult to establish, but rocks weighing up to 600lb (270kg) were reported at one crusader siege, although it seems likely that the norm was usually much less, possibly around 150lb (68kg). The range depended upon the capability of the machine and the size of the payload, but may have been up to 2-300 yards (183-274m). It should be noted that although trebuchets may have been capable of direct fire (ie, at an angle below 45 degrees) they normally operated like a modern howitzer, with the projectile describing a high arc (ie, between 45 and about 80 degrees), which was necessary to clear the castle walls, and then descending onto the target from above.

THE BALLISTA

In essence, the ballista was a giant crossbow mounted horizontally on a wooden platform, firing a large, metal-tipped wooden bolt. It was "cocked" by pulling back the string using pulleys until it engaged in a retaining device and was then released by some form of trigger. This was a direct fire, high velocity device and it is claimed that one particular model fired a bolt which could penetrate up to three men standing one behind the other.

LEFT: *A battering ram was more effective if the hole had been started by some other device, such as the two iron-tipped drills shown here. They could only be turned by hand or foot power and the operators would have had to be protected from hostile attack by timber roofs, unlike the men shown in this tranquil scene!*

RIGHT: The trebuchet, the precursor of today's howitzers, threw payloads into the besieged fortress, ranging from large rocks, through burning straw, to dead and decaying animals.

BELOW: Various weapons used in siege warfare, show that 13th and 14th Century engineers and artillerymen were considerably more ingenious than they are usually given credit for.

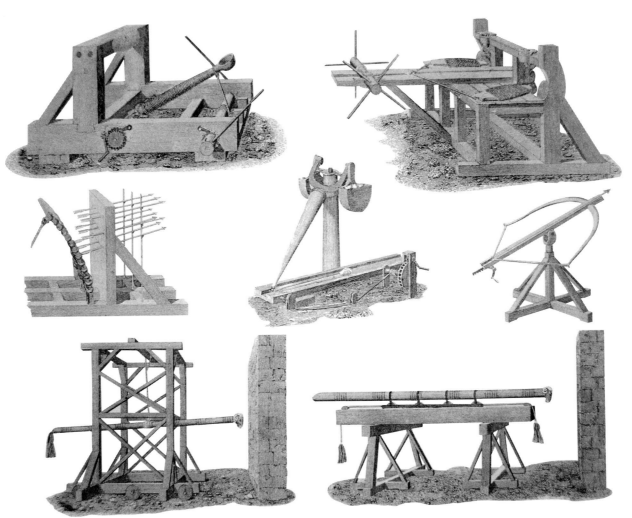

SAPPING AND MINING

Castle builders tried to prevent mining by surrounding a castle with a deep ditch or by building the foundations of the walls on rock. For the attackers, the most direct method of breaching such defences was to construct a sheltered surface approach (the "sap") to the foot of the wall and for the engineers ("sappers") then to dig out a cavern in the foundation of the wall. When deep enough, this cavern was shored with timbers and filled with combustible material. This was then ignited and (at least in theory) the props

Mining a fortress wall, where the attackers have dug a trench, protected by saps from attack from above. A bonfire would be lit to destroy temporary supporting timbers they have positoned.

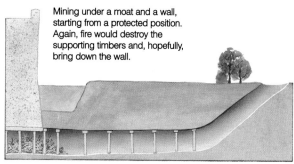

Mining under a moat and a wall, starting from a protected position. Again, fire would destroy the supporting timbers and, hopefully, bring down the wall.

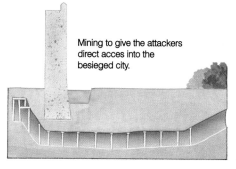

Mining to give the attackers direct acces into the besieged city.

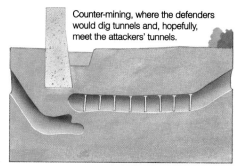

Counter-mining, where the defenders would dig tunnels and, hopefully, meet the attackers' tunnels.

would burn through and a section of the wall would collapse.

If this was impracticable then the next method was to dig a tunnel, starting at some distance from the wall. Some tunnels were extended past the foundations of the wall and used to infiltrate raiding parties. Others terminated in a chamber exactly underneath the walls. The chamber was propped up and filled with combustible materials, which were then fired, hopefully causing the walls above to collapse. One major problem with all tunnels is maintaining depth and direction, but it is not clear how this was achieved by the crusaders.

One of the disadvantages on creating a breach was that the wall or tower simply

BELOW: The ballista was a direct fire, high-velocity device and it is claimed that one particular model fired a bolt which could penetrate up to three men standing one behind the other.

collapsed downwards, leaving a great pile stones and masonry, and this was, in some ways, as great an obstacle as the original wall. At the siege of Acre this problem was so severe that Richard I offered massive sums to individuals brave enough to remove the debris and clear the way for the attackers.

MANTLETS

Among the simplest items of the attackers' equipment were mantlets, which were protective screens made of wood or wicker and behind which an archer or an observer could shelter. If light enough they could be carried; otherwise they were pushed on skids or rollers.

SCALING LADDERS

Walls were scaled using either Jacob's ladders (two ropes with rigid, wooden rungs) or wooden ladders. These were generally used in combination with other devices.

PALISADES

Both attackers and defenders would construct wooden palisades known as boulevards. For the defenders these were intended to provide an additional obstacle for the attackers, while the latter built them in order to prevent sallies by the besieged. In either case, the boulevard was effective only if it was manned and defended.

COUNTER-SIEGE WARFARE

GREEK FIRE

BELOW: A trebuchet launches a burning barrel into a castle, while infantry try to take the walls by storm from a siege tower and a ram is used in an attempt to break through the walls.

Greek Fire was the generic name for various incendiary devices, the original of which appears to have been invented by an Egyptian, but which was used principally by the Byzantines, for whom its composition was a closely guarded secret. Indeed, its actual nature remains a mystery to this day, but it is known that it was a gelatinous mixture and that its ingredients included saltpetre and pitch in a petroleum base. It was forced through copper tubes by a pump and appears to have ignited spontaneously on contact with air; it certainly could not be extinguished by water. The Arabs developed a naphtha-based substance with similar properties, and this was also known as "Greek Fire". From contemporary accounts it

would appear that the mixture was applied to a ball made of hemp or similar fibrous material, which immediately ignited and was then propelled towards the enemy using a catapult or ballista.

"Greek Fire" was normally used in sea battles but was also used in counter-siege warfare, particularly against siege towers. At the siege of Acre, for example, one of the crusaders' siege towers was hit by a fire bomb launched from a ballista and the whole tower and all the people inside were incinerated very quickly. As a result, the other two towers were hastily abandoned and were then destroyed by saracens in short order.

COUNTER-MINING

Obviously enemy mines (tunnelling) were a major concern to the defenders and efforts to prevent this started with clearing the ground around the castle so that the start of any mine could be seen. On occasions, mining activity was detected by placing basins of water over likely routes and watching for ripples, a primitive form of the modern seismograph. If a mine was either detected or suspected the defenders would often dig counter-mines with the aim of breaking into the enemy mine and then either attacking the miners, collapsing the tunnel, or, if water was available, flooding it. Such underground battles, almost invariably in darkness and accompanied by constant danger of the tunnel's collapse, were always particularly bloody and unpleasant.

BESIEGING THE BESIEGERS

One of the dangers for a besieging force was that of being attacked from the rear by a force coming to the relief of the besieged garrison. This happened during the siege of Acre in 1188-1191 when the crusader army prosecuting the siege was constantly harassed by Saladin's army which had taken up a position some three miles to its rear. The saracens carried out many minor and several major attacks before the crusaders eventually carried the fortress.

The saracen Nûr ad-Din was not so fortunate when he laid siege to the Krak des Chevaliers in 1163. Hearing of his attack, Count Raymond of Tripoli rapidly assembled a large crusader army which included forces under Count Hugh de Lusignan, Geoffrey Martel, Bohemond III Prince of Antioch, and even a Byzantine force under general Constantine Coloman. This army marched so quickly from the coast that it took Nûr ad-Din by surprise and after a short battle he abandoned the siege and retreated to Homs.

KRAK DES CHEVALIERS

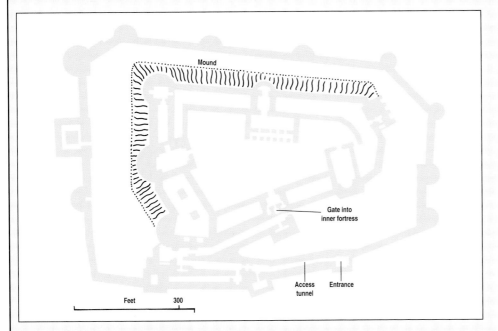

Mound

Gate into
inner fortress

Access   Entrance
tunnel

Feet   300

*LEFT: The Krak des
Chevaliers remains as one
of the greatest monuments
to the skill and
determination of the
crusaders, and in
particular to their
architects, engineers and
masons.*

One of the most famous castles in the world was built by the crusaders and remains in a remarkable state of preservation. It has had several names, one being. "Castle of the Kurds", from the origins of a one-time garrison, but it is under its crusader name of Krak des Chevaliers (castle of the knights) that it is known to history. The castle was built in a strategic position on top of a hill where its garrison could control the hinterland of Tripoli, restrict access to the River Orontes, and dominate the interior of Syria.

The present castle was built on the site of an earlier castle, which was first taken by a crusader force commanded by Raymond de St. Gillies, who occupied it briefly in 1099. He then lost it and besieged it again, this time unsuccessfully, in 1102. It was then recovered for the crusaders by Tancred in 1110 but in 1142 Raymond I, Count of Tripoli, passed it over to the Knights Hospitaller. It was unsuccessfully attacked by Nûr al-Dîn in 1163-64 and by the great Saladin for a month in 1184, but the crusaders held on to it until it finally fell to Sultan Baybars after a one- month siege on April 6, 1271. At the end of the siege the remaining few Knights Hospitaller were given safe conduct to Tripoli, but this last siege emphasid the necessity for an adequate garrison, since in the time of the Kurds the garrison was some 2,000, whereas when it was lost there were just 200 knights present.

The castle lies in an earthquake zone and is known to have been affected by quakes in 1157, 1170, 1201 and 1202, but there have undoubtedly been many others. Despite some minor damage, however, the mighty castle has survived them all.

It would appear that the castle was not built to a single coherent design but rather that it was the happy outcome of a combination of successful additions and modifications. It is constructed of closely hewn limestone blocks and is a concenrtric design, with an outer wall which includes 13 towers, most of them being semicircular with loopholes, and covering an area of some 6 acres (2.3 hectares). Within the shelter of the outer wall and partly underground are stables, barrackrooms for the garrison and storage chambers, and beneath these is another massive vault measuring some 200 by 300 feet (60 x 90m). It has been estimated that the various stores had sufficient capacity to support a garrison for some five years, had that been necessary.

One of the most interesting features was the mode of entry, which involved first crossing a drawbridge across a dry moat and then passing through a gateway protected by a portcullis. The visitor then found himself in a tunnel which turned sharp left and was straight and rising gradually for some 300ft (100m), the walls and roof containing small openings through which arrows could be fired or burning oil dropped on unwelcome visitors. The tunnel then turned 180 degrees with another straight stretch including more defensive devices. The chances of a group of enemies penetrating into the castle by this means were remote, to say the least.

The Krak des Chevaliers remains as a fitting and magnificent memorial to the anonymous designers and planners who produced many remarkable fortresses throughout the Holy Land.

THE SIEGE OF DARON

One of the more unusual examples of siege warfare was the taking of Daron in May 1192. Richard I was at the port of Ascalon when he suddenly decided to attack the Saracen fortress at Daron, some 30 miles (50km) further south along the coast. Always the man of action, he took a relatively small party of knights, some sixty according to one account, along the coast road, while more troops and the siege train followed by sea, although the bulk of the army remained at Ascalon.

When Richard and his knights arrived outside the fortress both attackers and defenders were astonished by the audacity of the undertaking, because the castle was strong and manned by a garrison of just under four hundred men. Seeing the disparity in their forces, the saracens immediately sortied out and challenged the impertinent crusaders to fight them, but Richard declined the invitation and waited on the beach for the slower sea convoy to arrive.

When the ships did arrive on the following day Richard was so hungry for action that he, his nobles and those knights not preventing the Turks from attacking them from the rear, doffed their armour and joined the labourers in carrying the heavy equipment from the boats and across the sands, and then assembling the engines. Richard then took personal command of one of the trebuchets, loading and aiming it himself. Such a striking example of leadership from the king was an inspiration to his troops and had a great impact on the Turks who were close enough to see what was going on.

On the fourth day the garrison sent out to offer terms, which Richard rejected with a message that they should fight like men. In the final assault some sixty saracens were killed and the remainder – just over 300 – plus their wives and children were sent into slavery. There

RIGHT: Defenders operate a device to harass the operators of a battering ram. The effect on the men inside must have been dreadful.

BELOW: The defenders were not powerless in the face of the attackers' siege train and its weaponry. Thus, battering rams could be resisted by the use of various barriers lowered from the battlements, such as a wicker-work screen, a wooden platform or a well-filled canvas blanket.

was no massacre on this occasion.

This small action, apart from demonstrating Richard I's leadership at its very best, also shows how necessary were the siege engines. Despite his daring and dash it would have been impossible for Richard's small force to have captured Daron without them.

Chapter 4

ARMOUR AND WEAPONS

T he crusades covered three centuries and the warriors came from various countries of central, western and northern Europe, so there were, naturally, many minor differences in their armour, dress, riding techniques and saddlery, and weapons, particularly in the early part of the period. As time went by, however, the crusaders not only learnt from each other, but they also took ideas from the saracens, whose clothing was, naturally, much more suited to the climate and local conditions. Thus, there were significant developments in both offensive and defensive capabilities, as well as a more coherent style of tactics, while the crusaders' dress, both for war and peace, became much better adapted to the hot climate. The three examples of crusader armour and weapons which follow cover the early, middle and later periods of the crusades but show only general styles, and it must be appreciated that there would have been many variations.

ABOVE: A contemporary picture of the First Crusade showing knights in chain mail, with helmets, shields and lances. They ride their destrier, or war-horses – their most valuable possessions.

THE KNIGHT
The basic element of the crusader armies was the knight (*chevalier*), a professional warrior, whose status and fighting abilities revolved around four essential elements: weapons, horses, attendants, and flags.

THE SWORD
The sword had three very important roles. First, it was the knight's principal weapon in close-quarter combat. Second, it was the symbol of the knight's membership of the warrior caste. Third, the similarity of its cruciform shape to that of the cross on which Jesus had died was seen to have a deep religious significance and the act of a knight raising his sword to his lips to kiss it had both a symbolic as well as a religious significance.

Swords were made in a wide variety of sizes and styles, and in the 11th Century were utilitarian and undecorated, although they became more elaborate as time passed, and a separate and more elaborate sword was developed for ceremonial use. For the war sword, ornamentation was of little significance and what mattered was its quality, especially its hardness and resilience.

HORSES

Apart from his sword, the most important symbols of the knight's status were his horses, which provided a mount in battle, a means of personal mobility in both war and peace, and a transport for his baggage. A knight would normally have, at the very least, two war-horses (*dexterarius* or *destrier*), at least one horse for riding off the battlefield (*palfrey* or *courser*), and several pack-horses (*sumpters*) to carry his belongings, but many would have had far more.

Horses supplied the primary means of mobility and transport for the knights, but they also imposed a significant logistic load on a crusader army. First, they required to be fed and watered regularly, failure to do so meaning that they became weaker and of increasingly less value in battle, posing particular problems in the desert terrain in which many campaigns were fought. Next, the horses required a modicum of care and attention, ande knig farriers were needed to keep them shod.

As time passed and the knight's armour became ever more effective against enemy weapons, the saracens learnt that it was more sensible to try to kill or wound the horse in order to force tht to dismount, at which stage he became virtually immobilised by his heavy armour and thus much easier to deal with. As a result, due to attrition in battle, by disease and as a result of starvation, horse losses were high and replacements (remounts) were required in large numbers. Finally, when moving by sea, the transportation of the horses was a much more demanding requirement, both in terms of space and the degree of care required, than that of moving the men.

BELOW: Duke Robert of Normandy rallies the crusaders while under attack from saracens during their trek across Anatolia. Note that the crusader columns were made up not just of knights and soldiers, but also of large numbers of pilgrims, including women and children.

ATTENDANTS

When a knight went to war he took with him a varying number of armed and mounted retainers, who formed his escort in battle. In addition, a knight also required a personal entourage, whose numbers depended upon his status and wealth, with four probably considered to be the minimum acceptable number. Of these, the most important was the esquire (from the French *escuyier*), who was responsible for the knight's weapons, especially the shield. The remaining three were responsible for a variety of tasks between them, including looking after the horses, helping the knight to mount his horse or to assist him if he was unhorsed in battle, and to guard prisoners, whose ransom money was a valuable source of income. In the 11th Century, such esquires (squires) were of low social status but during the course of the 12th and 13th Centuries their status increased, they became mounted and carried weapons, and eventually became eligible to become knights.

FLAGS

The fourth mark of distinction was the flag of which there were two varieties, both normally mounted at the tip of the lance to enable them to be seen from a distance. The pennon was pointed or forked and indicated an individual knight, while the banner was square in shape and indicated a baron or baronet in command of a group of at least ten knights.

These pennons and banners were emblazoned with their owner's armorial bearings as a means of recognition. Such bearings became hereditary and then a matter of family distinction and honour, giving rise to the complicated art of heraldry.

KNIGHTHOOD

The attainment of knighthood was not automatic and the aspiring knight had to meet three clearly understood conditions, which were birth, training, and age. First, under normal circumstances, only the sons of knights or of the nobility were eligible for knighthood, although exceptions could be made by the king in person. For training, the aspirant spent a period at the court of a noble, where he was trained in riding and the care of horses, the use of weapons, and the behaviour and courtesy expected of a knight. After reaching an acceptable standard, the aspiring knight was raised to the status of squire, which meant that he could take part in battles.

However, it was not until the squire had "come-of-age" on his twenty-first birthday

RIGHT: Two types of knight and a foot soldier at the time of the First Crusade (1096-99). Both knights have long chain mail coats, but while the man in the centre wears chain-mail leggings, the man on the right has no protection at all below the knees. The unfortunate foot soldier has no body protection at all, apart from a chain-mail cap and a small shield.

(and provided that he met all the other criteria) that he became eligible to be raised to the status of knight by his master. This ceremony of "dubbing" had a strong religious flavour and was full of symbolism. Although there were many minor variations, the ceremony usually started in the evening before the ceremony when the candidate went to church where he made an act of confession which was followed by a penance, normally consisting of a lengthy vigil of prayer and fasting. This ended with a ritual bath, indicating the final washing away of sins, following which he donned a white surcoat, signifying a new purity of spirit. During the actual ceremony the aspirant knelt in the presence of other knights and clergy and pronounced the vow of chivalry, following which the "god-father" touched the new knight lightly on each shoulder in turn with a sword (the "dubbing"). During all this the aspirant's own sword had been blessed by a priest and left lying on the altar, until everything else had been completed, at which time the sword was presented to the new knight who held it in both hands and kissed the pommel to signify his faith to "the Cross" and his dedication to life as a knight.

TWELFTH CENTURY ARMOUR AND EQUIPMENT

ARMOUR

During the period of the early Crusades (ie, at the end of the 12th Century) the Latin knight was dressed in the manner familiar from depictions in the Bayeaux tapestry. His primary weapons were the lance and sword, and his means of protection a chain-mail outfit, with a low crowned helmet and a kite-shaped shield. This outfit had been developed over centuries of warfare in northern and western Europe and made no allowances for the heat and humidity of the eastern Mediterranean. The main outfit was made of chain-mail which, although fairly heavy and none too effective in close-quarter combat, was very flexible

The knight's innermost layer of protection was the gambeson, a tunic made of quilted cotton material, with long sleeves, what would be described in modern terms as a "crew neck", and a split skirt extending down to the knees. Over this was worn a hauberk, a tunic fabricated from a single piece of chain-mail with a skirt down to the knees, a built-in coif (head-covering), and long sleeves with lace ties at the wrist. The hands were protected by separate chain-mail mittens with lace wrist-ties and soft leather lining for the palms, to provide a proper grip for weapons.

The built-in coif was fabricated from chain-mail with a soft leather lining to prevent chafing and had a leather binding around the edge of the face-piece. The coif included the aventail, a form of flap, also of leather-lined chain-mail, which was used to cover the lower face, and which could either be left open or pulled across and secured with a lace tie near the left ear. When this was fully closed only the knight's upper cheeks, eyes and nose were exposed.

ABOVE: A 12th Century depiction of three crusader knights, showing their very long, pointed shields and long, chain-mail coats.

The knight then donned a helmet that was normally a spangenhelm, either hemispherical or slightly conical in shape. Made of iron, this consisted of a circular frame with four arches to which were rivetted four shaped iron segments. The inside of the helmet had a leather lining. The most obvious visual characteristic was the "nasal" (nose guard) which extended below the front of the helmet to cover the wearer's nose. Sometimes this was a simple strip, but in more sophisticated versions it was three-dimensional, covering both the front and sides of the nose. The helmet was held in place by lace ties passing under the chin.

The knight wore cotton breeches, secured by a waist-band, and woolen stockings. His legs and thighs were then covered with chausses (chain-lined leggings) which were held up by ties to the waist-band of his breeches. The leggings had integral foot coverings, with the soles of the feet protected by a leather lining. Finally, spurs were secured around the ankles.

The chain-mail hauberk was fabricated from between 200,000 and 300,000 separate metal links and weighed approximately 25lb (11kg). The construction of the chain-mail enabled the knight to be fairly mobile and it was effective at a distance, but it could be penetrated by the sharp point of an arrowhead or of a spear, and it gave way under a blow from a sword. This was the reason for the gambeson, which was needed to absorb the shock of a sword, while the shield would, it was hoped, prevent arrows or spears reaching their targets.

BELOW: A contemporary illustration of a late 13th Century knight, who, apart from the gap for his face, is totally covered in chain-mail, even including his hands. Note the pointed spurs and leather facing on the palms of his hand covering.

WEAPONS

The mounted knight's primary weapon was the spear, which consisted of a wooden shaft some 8-9ft (2.5-2.8m) long with a pointed iron head. Next came the sword, which was suspended from a leather sword-belt worn outside the hauberk. The sword consisted of a long iron or steel blade with a short, leather-covered handle. Most knights also carried a short, simple dagger.

The shield at this period was that commonly associated with William the Conqueror's Norman army, being a kite-shaped device made of wood, covered with leather and with an iron boss. There were three straps: two enarmes for the knight's arm to hold the shield in the fighting position, and one guige to sling the shield around his neck and shoulder when not in combat. The shape of the shield resulted from the need to protect the mounted knight from his eyes down to his feet – thus the top was rounded and the bottom tapered to a point.

HERALDRY

During this period of the crusades heraldry was fairly elementary and extended to a simple banner on the lance, painting on the face of the shield, and the colouring of the helmet. Some knights also tied long-tailed scarves around their helmets.

Thirteenth Century Armour and Equipment

By the middle and late 13th Century the crusaders had started to incorporate the lessons of their many campaigns. Protection was generally greater, usually by adding extra layers to cover critical areas, such as the abdomen, arms, and legs. The helmet was also more substantial.

Armour

The innermost upper garment was the aketon, a tunic made of quilted cotton, with long sleeves and a low crew-neck collar. Outside this was the cuirass, made of thick cotton with built-in hardened leather plates to give additional protection. When laid flat the cuirass formed a cruciform, with the longer arm including a round hole for the head, while the shorter arm went around the abdomen and was secured by straps at the rear.

The head protection had now changed significantly in character. There was a separate inner quilted coif covering the head and ears, and this was held in place by a cloth tie passing under the chin. Over this was worn a chain-mail coif – now separated from the haubergeon – with a wide tippet, which spread over the wearer's shoulders to give protection against a downward slash. There was still an aventail secured above the left ear to protect the mouth and jaw. There were now, however, different styles of mail coif, which incorporated various types of padding to support the different types of helmet which had been introduced.

The great helm was a large, pot-shaped device covering the entire head and neck, the only openings being narrow vision slits, while perforations in the lower part aided ventilation. This offered much greater protection and, since it rested on the wearer's crown, it was more comfortable to wear. It did, however, have the disadvantages of possessing a very limited field of view, as well as being heavy and hot.

The second type of helmet, the chapel-de-fer, consisted of a hemispherical headpiece, with a wide brim, which offered a shade from the sun and also served to deflect downward blows. In fact, it had a remarkable resemblance to the steel helmet worn by British and United States soldiers during World War I.

Below the waist the knight wore cotton hose under the chauses (mail leggings) which included an integral shoe, again with a leather sole. Protection could be improved by adding conical poleyns to protect the knees, which were sewn onto a tubular quilted cuisse to hold them in place.

ABOVE: A 13th Century
French knight, as shown in a
contemporary manuscript. The
horse has no protection at all,
but note the high front and
rear pieces of the wood-and-
leather saddle. The knight is
not carrying a shield, possibly
simply an oversight on the
part of the artist.

WEAPONS

By now swords had improved considerably in quality and greater use was being made of steel. In general a knight would have a war sword for use when mounted and a shorter sword for use on foot, both of which were plain and utilitarian, and possibly a more elaborate, richly decorated sword for use on ceremonial occasions. The sword could be suspended from the waist belt, as before, but the baldric, a sling passing over the right shoulder, had also been introduced. Daggers had also become more elaborate and were widely used. Maces were also carried, usually consisting of a wooden handle some 28-32in (70-80cm) long, and a heavy iron head, usually segmented.

The mounted knight had much better protection for his legs, which meant that the bottom of the shield could be made shorter and cut straight. Also, since better facial protection was provided by the vizor, the top of the shield could also be straightened. In combination, this resulted in a more rectangular shield.

HERALDRY

Because the helmet now completely covered the knight's face he needed some form of identification which was provided by heraldic devices on the helmet, surcoat and shield.

FOURTEENTH CENTURY ARMOUR AND EQUIPMENT

ARMOUR

LEFT: An English chain-mail
shirt of the 13th Century.
Making such an intricate
device would have required
painstaking care on the part of
the blacksmith.

The basic garment was still the gambeson over which was worn a cuirass (also known as a "coat-of-plates"), a one-piece garment through which the wearer placed his head and then tied back the two side pieces. The garment itself consisted of iron plates attached by rivets to a soft leather backing, and with a decorative outer cover, sometimes of velvet. Over this was worn the chain-mail haubergeon and on top of that a surcoat sometimes decorated with fancy embroidery depicting the

ABOVE: The upper panel shows a French knight (seated in cart, centre) with his entourage of squires, servants and pack animals. The carts carry tents, cooking equipment and clothes.

RIGHT: A 13th Century French knight prepares to ride into battle, assisted by his squire (kneeling), page (standing, with helmet) and groom (background, with spear).

ARMOUR AND WEAPONS 89

wearer's heraldic device. The surcoat was not, however, worn for its decorative effect, but because it served to keep the wearer much cooler than if his chain-mail hauburgeon was outermost.

Headwear had become even more complex. Innermost was a cerevillière, a metal inner helmet with a padded lining. Over this went a chain-mail coif with a wide tippet and over that a bascinet, a heavy helmet with low sides and rear to protect the neck, and a visor which closed, leaving a small slit for the eyes. This could be topped by a crest, featuring a device associated with the wearer.

Again, the protection afforded to the limbs was increased, principally by the addition of strap-on plates, such as rerebraces and vamabraces for the upper and lower arms. The same applied to the legs, with mail chausses for the thigh, hardened leather greaves for the shins, and poleyns for the knees. At the same time mittens had given way to gauntlets made of articulated armoured plate sown onto a leather liner, with a wide cuff providing protection for the wrist.

ABOVE: Various medieval war hammers and maces which would have been used in close-quarter combat.

WEAPONS

The main improvement in the sword was in quality resulting from enhancements in steel-making, which also enabled the sword to be somewhat larger without any loss of strength. The spear, which was now more properly termed a lance, had also become more substantial and longer – some 10-11ft (3.0-3.4m) – and incorporated a graper (collar) which was intended to fit forward of the armpit, thus preventing the spear from riding back under the shock of impact with an enemy. Apart from the usual pointed iron head for use in mounted engagements, a special type of lance with a hooked blade was used in siege warfare, being used by knights atop belfries to snag defenders on the battlements and pull them off. Shields remained made of wood with a leather covering and some introduced a slot in the upper right quadrant (viewed from the inside) which served as a rest for the lance.

FOOT SOLDIERS

Some foot soldiers came from the crusaders' home countries, but most were mercenaries, either from Italy or locally recruited among Syrians and Turcopoles. There are very few records of what the foot soldiers wore, and, in any case, it is unlikely that there was any uniformity, the men being left to obtain what they could through capture on the field, purchase or gambling. However, they were generally divided into spearmen or crossbowmen and their dress would have been very simple, consisting of a long-sleeved cotton shirt over which was a quilted aketon. The helmet was a simple conical device, perhaps with a brim, and most foot soldiers were armed with a short sword, a light spear, and a kite-shaped or circular shield. Bowmen would have carried their bow, usually a crossbow and a supply of quarrels. It is likely that only the shield was marked with any form of identifying device, although some contingents may have worn particular coloured shirts to aid identification in battle.

HORSE FURNITURE

As described above, the war-horse (*destrier*) was the essential symbol of the knight's status and was, therefore, well looked after. The basic harness was little different from that found today, but saddle seats were a mixture of leather and wood, while the front and rear pieces were made of wood and designed to keep the knight on the horse's back, as well as to provide protection, particularly in the front. The saddle was held in place by a breast-strap and a girth (sometimes a double girth) passing under the horse, and secured by either a buckle or leather laces. Stirrups, made of bronze or steel were suspended from the saddle by leather straps.

The saracens quickly learned that the best way to deal with a crusader knight was to kill or wound his horse. The crusaders countered this by developing for their horses an armoured coat, usually of chain-mail. This, in turn, was sometimes covered by a surcoat. A protective head-piece, known as a *chamfron*, could be either an integral part of the armoured coat or separate, and consisted of a padded lining and an armoured covering of either hardened leather or iron plates, with holes for the ears and eyes. The nostrils and mouth were left free.

SARACEN ARMOUR AND EQUIPMENT

ARMOUR

The basic equipment worn by the saracen horseman was very similar to that of the crusaders; indeed, from a distance there were more similarities than there were differences, although the saracens did not use the "great helm" adopted by the crusaders later in the period.

The undergarments were made of cotton and consisted of a loose-fitting tunic and drawers with a draw-string, as was necessary in a hot climate. Over this was worn a protective garment, either a lamellar cuirass or a chain-mail hauberk. The hauberk, known as a *dir*, was generally similar to that worn by the crusaders, except that the collar was higher, being raised by means of a leather stiffener to provide additional protection to the throat and neck. In some cases the sleeves were long, but in others they were elbow length, in order to give more freedom when using a

bow. The cuirass, known as a *jawshan*, was made of supple leather with either hardened leather or iron lamellas attached. On his legs the horseman wore leggings made of leather or padded cotton, and leather riding boots; some, but not all, had spurs.

The saracen rider's head was protected by a helmet, usually of iron although leather was also sometimes used. The helmet was secured by leather ties under the chin and, in many cases, had a turban tied around it so that only the top of the helmet could be seen.

All shields were made from wood, with a hard leather covering, and were normally painted, but there were many variations in size and shape. Most horsemen seem to have carried circular shields held by means of leather straps; the larger version was known as a *turs*, while the much smaller one was a *duraqah*. Some Saracen horsemen seem to have adopted the crusader kite-shaped shields (*tariqah*), although these were most probably captured on the battlefield, a source of equipment and weapons used by both sides.

WEAPONS

The main offensive weapon was the bow, which was recurvate in profile (ie, a double S-shape) and of composite construction, being made from a mixture of wood, horn and sinew. Taken in combination, these meant that the pull reduced as the bow was extended, thus making it easy to aim. Compared with crusader weapons, the saracen recurved bow was more accurate and had a longer range than the longbow, but lacked the penetrating power of the crossbow.

As with the Japanese samurai, the saracens developed a remarkable variety of arrowheads, designed to meet different requirements, such as use against cavalry or infantry, against targets with or without armour (and, if so, what types of armour), against horses, and so on.

The main weapon for close-quarter use was the sword. Horsemen used the characteristic curved sword, while infantry used the old-fashioned straight sword. The saracens set particular store by their maces, which were usually about 3ft (1m) long and consisted of a wooden shaft with an iron head. Other weapons included axes, daggers, knives, spears and, occasionally, javelins.

ABOVE: A heavily armed and armoured crusader knight in combat with a much more lightly equipped and armed (and thus much more agile) saracen horseman.

RIGHT: A saracen pole-axe, which was not only a highly effective and much feared weapon, but also, with its symmetrical design and intricate scroll-work, a work of art.

RIGHT: A saracen sword with an unusual bifurcated tip. Arab sword makers were greatly helped by the excellence of the metal they worked with, especially the Damascene steel from Damascus.

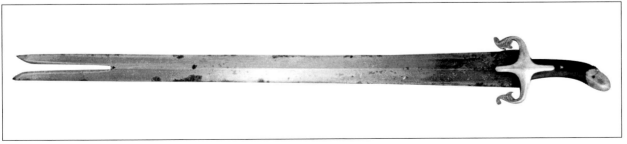

Chapter 5

THE BATTLE OF THE HORNS OF HATTIN

The Battle of the Horns of Hattin on July 3/4, 1187, was an almost total victory for the great Saladin, since only a tiny proportion of the enemy escaped, and all the rest were either killed or captured. Even though Saladin showed consummate generalship, however, the crusaders contributed greatly to their own defeat through the bitterness of their internecine quarrels and the incompetence of their leaders.

The chain of events leading to this battle started with the death of King Baldwin IV of Jerusalem, who succumbed to leprosy in 1185. He was succeeded by his young nephew, Baldwin V, with Raymond of Tripoli as regent, but the new king died after only a year on the throne, leaving something of a vacuum. A powerful courtier, Joscelin of Courtenay, seized the opportunity and persuaded Raymond to meet a group of barons at Tiberias, but then, with Raymond safely out of the way, Joscelin arranged the coronation of Baldwin IV's sister, Princess Sibylla, who promptly gave the crown to her husband, Guy of Lusignan. Raymond and many of the barons were indignant, but they had been completely outmanoeuvred and they were forced to either accept the situation, albeit with ill grace, or to leave the country.

A four-year truce with Saladin had recently come into force and was carefully observed by both sides, but proved to be of particular benefit to the crusaders as trade and prosperity increased. But one of the crusader nobles, Reynald de Châtillon, provided the random act that so often has consequences far beyond anything the originator intended. Reynald ruled an area in Oultrejourdain to the southeast of the Dead Sea from his magnificent castle at Kerak, but was noted for his arrogance, rash acts and wanton cruelty, even in a community where none of these characteristics was in short supply. This man, probably through greed, carried out an unprovoked and bloody attack on a particularly large and wealthy Muslim caravan that was passing near Kerak, an act which was in direct contravention of the truce.

BELOW: The routes that the crusaders and the saracens followed, in their apparently inexorable progress towards their great confrontation at the Horns of Hattin in July 1187.

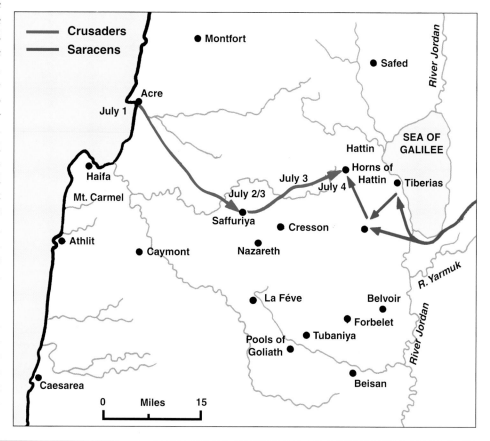

Saladin sent emissaries demanding immediate release of the hostages and the payment of compensation; Reynald refused to meet the embassy, who then went to see King Guy. The king, however, was a weak man and, in any case, he owed his position to Reynald, so did nothing. Not surprisingly, Saladin decided that he had no alternative but to invade and, on receiving news of this, King Guy also assembled his forces.

Some sort of mediation might just have been possible at this stage, but an incident then occurred which made war inevitable. On April 30, 1187, a party of some seven thousand mamelukes were watering their horses at the Springs of Cresson when they were seen by a group of crusader knights, fewer than two hundred strong, led by the Grand Master of the Temple, James de Mailly, and the Grand Master of the Hospitallers, Roger de Les Moulins. Despite the overwhelming strength of the saracens, the various factions in the crusader group taunted each other until they had no choice but to undertake a very rash attack, in which the crusaders were virtually annihilated. Only three Templars escaped, of whom Gerard de Ridefort, Grand Master of the Templars and the man primarily responsible for starting the attack, was one. But, with this incident, war was now unavoidable.

THE ARMIES

CRUSADERS

The numerical strength of any group in the medieval period is always difficult to establish because methods of counting at the time were very imprecise. However, it seems a reasonable estimate that at the Battle of Hattin the crusader army was about 20,000 strong. The mounted component comprised some 1,200 heavy cavalry (knights), of which about one-quarter were Templars, one-quarter Hospitallers, and the remaining half lay barons and

RIGHT: Members of the Order of the Knights Templar. Their Grand Master played a crucial role in persuading the king to fight at Hattin – which proved to be a major, and very tragic, error.

knights, together with some 4,000 light cavalry, a mixture of Christian sergeants and locally enlisted turcopoles. There was a much larger number of infantry, of widely varying quality, probably numbering about 15,000. The crusader army also included a large number of priests and two bishops, who brought with them their most treasured religious relic, a portion of the "True Cross", as an encouragement for the crusaders.

The crusader army was, in fact, the largest they had assembled up to that time, and for the brief campaign that was about to take place it was organised into three "guards". The leading body, the "vanguard", was commanded, as was customary, by the seigneur of the country through which they were passing, which in this case was Raymond III, Count of Tripoli. Next came the main guard, commanded by King Guy, and this included two bishops carrying the "True Cross". Finally, there was the rear guard, commanded by a redoubtable warrior, Balian d'Ibelin, which included contingents of Templars and Hospitallers. The rear guard was considered to be the position of both the greatest danger and the greatest honour, since it was known that one of the main saracen tactics was to try to detach it from the main body and then gradually wear it down.

SARACENS

The saracen army was considerably stronger, perhaps 45-50,000 in all, and was under Saladin's personal command. It was a heterogeneous collection of contingents, which included Mameluke regiments from Egypt, Syrian archers, Turkoman horse-archers, and many others. As always with saracen armies it included a large number of "musicians" with drums, timbrels, trumpets, gongs and rattles, whose task was to generate a vast volume of noise, which was considered to encourage the fighting troops and to demoralise the enemy. Saladin divided his army into three major divisions: the right wing under his nephew, Taqi al-Din, the left wing under Gökböri, while Saladin himself was in overall command, as well as in direct command of the centre division.

PRELIMINARY MOVES

SARACENS

The saracens took up a position on the high ground to the south of Lake Tiberias around the village of Kafr Sabt, where there were several wells. This was about six miles (8km) away from Tiberias to the east and a similar distance from the crusader camp at Saffuriya to the west.

Saladin's plan was to use part of his force to attack the crusader fortress at Tiberias, which was being held by a garrison commanded by Countess Eschiva, whose husband, Count Raymond of Tripoli, was with Guy's army. This would, Saladin hoped, force Raymond and others to urge King Guy to take his army to the rescue, whereupon Saladin would attack the lumbering, slow-moving crusader army as it crossed the open and waterless plain of Lubiya, using his much more mobile and closely controlled army. An added advantage was that Saladin had well-placed spies in the crusader camp who kept him informed of the endless dissension among the upper echelons of the crusader leadership.

The preliminary moves went precisely as planned, with Saladin leading the attack on Tiberias in person. The city was taken on July 2, leaving Countess Eschiva and a small garrison trapped inside the citadel, following which, as Saladin had predicted, the countess despatched a messenger to the king with a plea for help. Needless to say, the saracens took great care to ensure that the messenger was allowed to reach his destination.

BELOW: By the night of July 3/4 (top) the crusaders had lost the initiative, were surrounded and were desperately thirsty. On July 4 matters became much worse and by mid-day (bottom) Raymond had involuntarily led his cavalry off the battlefield, while the infantry was heading for the high ground.

The message from Countess Eschiva arrived at dusk on July 2 and King Guy immediately called a council-of-war in his royal marquee, but a host of problems ensured that matters did not proceed smoothly. First, as was almost always the case with the crusaders, there was marked and long-standing animosity between some of the leaders. Second, King Guy was a weak man and poor leader, who owed his crown to the fact that he had married the daughter of the previous king and who had an alarming tendency to agree with the last person to have spoken to him. Third, there were a lot of people present; the actual number has never been established, but was almost certainly in the region of several hundred, although only a few of the most senior men were allowed to speak.

After some preliminaries, Count Raymond addressed the meeting: he was the most powerful landowner present; the city under siege, Tiberias, was his; and the lady trapped in the citadel was his wife. But, to everyone's surprise he advocated not going to her rescue, because he sensed a trap. Saladin, he argued, was a chivalrous man who would not harm a Christian lady, and it was all part of a plan to get the crusader army into open, where he would attack and defeat it on a waterless plain. Raymond, of course, knew the local countryside well, which lent strength to his argument, and he finished by suggesting that the crusader army should remain in its present position, leaving Saladin to decide whether to withdraw or to attack them.

Raymond was mistrusted by some of those present, but his eloquence and reasoning won the day and the meeting broke up with an agreement to stay put for the time being. All then returned to their tents, except for the Grand Master of the Templars, Gerard de Ridefort, who remained with the king in an attempt to make him change his mind. Gerard suggested that Raymond, who spoke fluent Arabic and had met most of the Muslim leaders, must be in league with Saladin; how else could he be so confident that his wife would be safe? Also, Gerard pointed out that if King Guy was seen to fail to go to the aid of a city just 12 miles (19km) away he would lose respect throughout both Outremer and Europe. Finally, Gerard played his trump card, telling Guy that if he failed to act the Templars would withdraw their support, not only for the current expedition but also for Guy's continuance on the throne. Weakly, Guy gave in and

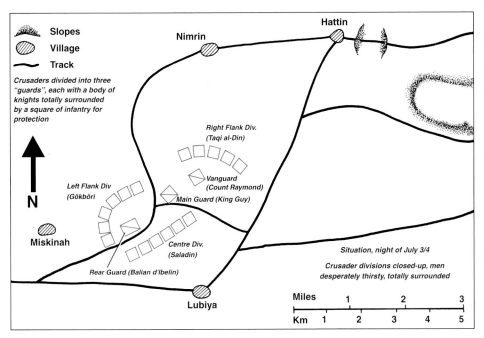

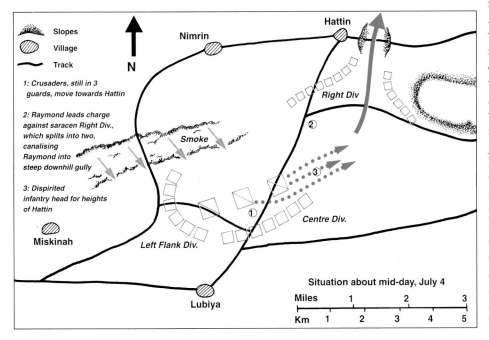

trumpeters were sent around the camp to announce that the army would march to Tiberias at dawn. The knights were amazed and alarmed by the change of plan, since the dangers of marching across the waterless plain in the summer heat had been spelt out so clearly by Raymond. Nevertheless, they complied with Guy's orders and the army marched at first light, at which the observers posted by Saladin withdrew to report to their master.

JULY 3, 1187

Saladin was still at Tiberias when he received the message that the crusaders were on the march and he immediately returned to his headquarters at Kafr Sabt. Even before he had arrived, however, his two subordinates, Taqi al-Din and Gökböri, had sent out patrols of light cavalry with instructions to harass the crusaders but not attack in such strength that they stopped them heading for Tiberias.

THE CRUSADER ARMY ON THE MOVE

As the crusader army advanced in three divisions, it was known that the saracens would concentrate their efforts on killing or wounding the crusader horses in order to bring down the knights who, once on foot, were very slow moving and highly vulnerable. As a result, the crusaders had developed the tactic of very close cooperation, with the knights moving forward surrounded by a square of infantry. The bowmen and crossbowmen were also tasked to concentrate their fire on enemy horsemen to keep them at bay. All this meant that the columns moved extremely slowly, its speed of advance probably being no more than two miles per hour (3kmh).

One problem began to influence the crusaders from early in the day – a shortage of water, which had not been helped by an order from King Guy that the usual water carts were to be left behind; thus, each man had only his leather water-bottle to depend on. The columns set out just before dawn, but the men began to feel increasingly tired and threatened as the heat built up, water ran out, the pressure from constant saracen attacks increased, and the continuous beating of saracen war-drums and rattles began to wear the crusaders down mentally. By mid-morning, after they had been marching for some five to six hours, all were beginning to suffer from exhaustion and thirst.

Guy's army veered east into the Wadi Rummanah and approached Mount Turan where it was known that there was a well, and many had drunk their water in anticipation of refilling them there. But, for reasons never recorded, the army pressed on without stopping, which proved to be a major blunder. By late morning Raymond in the advance guard wanted to increase the pace to reach Lake Tiberias sooner, but the column was now spread out, everyone was suffering from the heat, and the rate of progress had slowed to a crawl. In addition, harassment of the rear guard by the saracen light horse had now reached such an intensity that a message was sent to Guy requesting a halt to enable the knights to charge the enemy and drive them away.

Guy felt that he had no choice and ordered a halt, which angered Raymond who wanted to push on. But at this point King Guy made a change to his previous plan and decided to head northeast across the desert to the spring at Kafr Hattin, which was some three to four miles 5-6km) away, where they would halt for the night and then reach Lake Tiberias the following day. Up to this point discipline had been reasonably good but with the change of direction and the prospect of water before them, some of the knights now broke away from the infantry and pressed on towards the wells. Raymond and the advance guard swung towards the northeast, as ordered, and found Taqi's forces in front of them, preventing access to the springs. Raymond was preparing to charge with his knights when he suddenly received an order from Guy to halt for the night. Raymond was furious and wanted to charge through the enemy ranks regardless of the cost, but could not do so against the king's orders.

SARACEN MANOEUVRES

During this day Saladin had been in no hurry as he watched the crusaders conform to what he expected and he fed his army very gradually into the fight, thus maintaining constant pressure on the enemy. Then, as soon as he saw the knights pull out to hurry towards the springs at Hattin, he ordered his commanders, Gökböri and Taqi al-Din, to move to block the crusaders' path, while he continued to hold the high ground at Kafr Sabt. This was done and the crusaders were forced to make camp in the open.

NIGHT

As night fell the position was that the crusaders were camped on the plain – hot, hungry, thirsty, angry and confused. The saracens were camped very close-by, confident and looking forward to the morrow, while they were resupplied with ample stocks of water, brought by camels from Lake Tiberias, and their supply of arrows was replenished by stocks brought by dromedary from the forward supply depot at Kafr Sabt. Also during the night, parties of

RIGHT: The end at the Horns of Hattin, with the main body of the crusaders making a futile last stand on top of the "horns". Balian d'Ibelin and a few knights from the rearguard were the only crusaders to escape. Saladin's victory was complete.

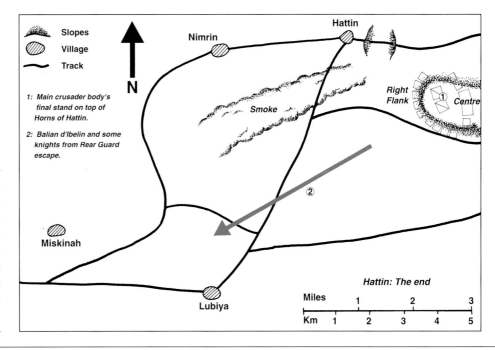

Slopes
Village
Track

N

1: Main crusader body's final stand on top of Horns of Hattin.

2: Balian d'Ibelin and some knights from Rear Guard escape.

Nimrin

Hattin

Right Flank

Smoke

Centre

①

②

Miskinah

Lubiya

Hattin: The end

Miles   1   2   3

Km   1   2   3   4   5

Saracen labourers gathered large stocks of dry brushwood, which would be used to great advantage the following day.

July 4, 1187

After a very uncomfortable night the crusader army assembled just before dawn and then set out in the same formations as the previous day and under the same commanders, towards their first goal, the springs at the village of Hattin, which were some three miles distant. From the start the saracens constantly harassed the crusaders, trying, as always, to isolate the rearguard, but on this day they introduced a new element by setting fire to piles of brushwood, which had been carefully sited so that the acrid smoke blew down on the crusader columns. This caused the men to close up on each other in confusion, while also hiding the advancing saracens from view; the acrid smoke also, of course, made the crusaders' thirst even worse.

The fighting became general but then, without any warning, the morale of the crusader infantry cracked and they started to head in large numbers up the slopes towards the two hills known as the Horns of Hattin. King Guy was unable to prevent this and in an effort to restore order he pitched his red tent to serve as a rallying point. But the infantry continued to head up the hill, even though knights rode through them, trying to persuade them to return to the main body.

In the vanguard Raymond saw what was going on and realised that the day was almost

lost. He was then ordered by the king to take the knights of the vanguard and to charge the saracen division commanded by Taqi al-Din which had been sited to screen off the springs at Hattin. Raymond led his men in a wild charge, heading straight for the saracen forces. But Taqi al-Din, a most perceptive commander, realised at once that the charge was unstoppable, so he simply opened up a large gap in his ranks, allowing Raymond and his crusaders to ride straight through, where their momentum led them into a gorge leading down into the valley. As soon as the crusaders had passed through, Taqi closed his ranks behind them, and because of the narrowness and steepness of the gorge, and the strength in which the top was being held, it was impossible for Raymond and his knights to fight their way back up again. Some historians have suggested that Raymond considered that all was lost and was simply trying to escape, but this seems very unlikely. Whatever the explanation, Raymond and his men had no choice but to keep going and to depart.

Back on the hill, the great mass of the crusader infantry now drifted onto the northern Horn and milled around sullenly, refusing to take any further part in the battle, while below them the main group of knights around Guy's tent decided to try to kill Saladin and charged twice. The first time they got within a stone's throw of the enemy commander's tent before being forced back, and the second charge got so close that Saladin had to use his sword to protect himself. Down at the rear-guard the knights of the military orders made repeated charges to try to break the saracens' grip, but to no avail, although when it was quite clear that all was lost a few knights in the rear guard managed to escape, led by Balian d'Ibelin. Then Taqi and his men captured the "True Cross" and the battle was quickly over. Curiously, despite the desperate nature of the fighting and although there were some casualties, particularly among the military orders, and despite heavy losses among the horses, the great majority of knights survived without serious wounds.

AFTERMATH

The saracens were quick to sort things out in the aftermath of victory. The crusader foot soldiers were rounded up into groups, chained together, and led away to slavery. Indeed, so many of them were placed on the market simultaneously that the price collapsed and slaves were changing hands for the price of a pair of sandals.

Things were different for the knights. Reynald de Châtillon, who had proved such a cruel scourge of Muslims for so many years and whose unjustified attack on the caravan had provoked this particular war, was struck down in Saladin's tent, possibly by the Muslim commander in person, and his execution completed by a nearby soldier. Then on the following day all the captured Hospitallers and Templars – some 230 all told – were executed at Saladin's orders, precisely the same fate that the crusaders would have meted out to captured Muslims. Somewhat ironically, however, the Grand Master, whose military advice to Guy had been directly responsible for this disaster, was the only one to be spared. That left several hundred knights, including King Guy, who were imprisoned and later ransomed.

CONCLUSION

In this battle Saladin achieved every general's greatest aim in that he fought against his enemy's main force, on ground and at a time of his own choosing, and achieved a virtually total victory, since only a handful of the enemy escaped. For the crusaders it was a complete military disaster brought about by poor planning and bad tactics, aggravated by squabbling and dissension among the commanders.

Although often overlooked as a factor in medieval warfare, it should be noted that logistics played a significant role for both sides. For the crusaders it was lack of water that was the most serious for the men and probably, although not mentioned in the history books, for the horses, as well. On the other side, the saracen resupply arrangements worked brilliantly, with an abundance of water and arrows being brought up during the night of July 3/4, the well-organized columns of camels and other animals bringing the supplies forward to where they were needed.

The saracens also proved themselves adept at what would today be termed "psychological warfare". The constant noise preyed on the crusader soldiers' minds, while the ostentatious way in which the saracen soldiers poured away their excess drinking water on the morning of July 4 must have been very galling. Then, too, there was the use of smoke, which added to the sense of confusion and disorientation.

LEFT: The city of Jerusalem, from a woodcut in the "Liber Chronicarum Mundi" published in Nuremberg, Germany, in 1493.

Chapter 6

THE SIEGE OF ACRE

Acre, whose full crusader name was St. Jeanne d'Acre, was the greatest city on the coast of the Holy Land, located some 30 miles (48km) south of Tyre. It was first captured by the crusaders in 1104 and was then held by them for 83 years, becoming a very prosperous trading centre. The city was built on a low-lying promontory and on the two landward sides it was protected by an immensely strong, 90-foot (27m) high wall, with the added protection of a 30-foot (9m) deep ditch, designed to prevent siege engines from approaching too closely. The wall consisted of two essentially straight sections, meeting at an acute angle at the northeast corner of the city, this junction-point being guarded by the Maledicta tower (the Tower of the Accursed).

The harbour was entirely man-made, having been created by building a mole as an extension of the eastern wall, at the seaward end of which was the Tower of the Flies. This tower dominated the entrance to the Outer Harbour, and there was a further entrance to the Inner Harbour, protected by a chain. Inside the walls the city was a warren of narrow, winding streets with an exceptional number of churches, numerous markets, plus palaces belonging to the Hospitallers, the Templars and the richer merchants. The seaward side of the city was also

ABOVE: *The court of King Godfrey of Jerusalem, the immediate predecessor to King Guy, showing an idyllic existence which bore little relation with reality.*

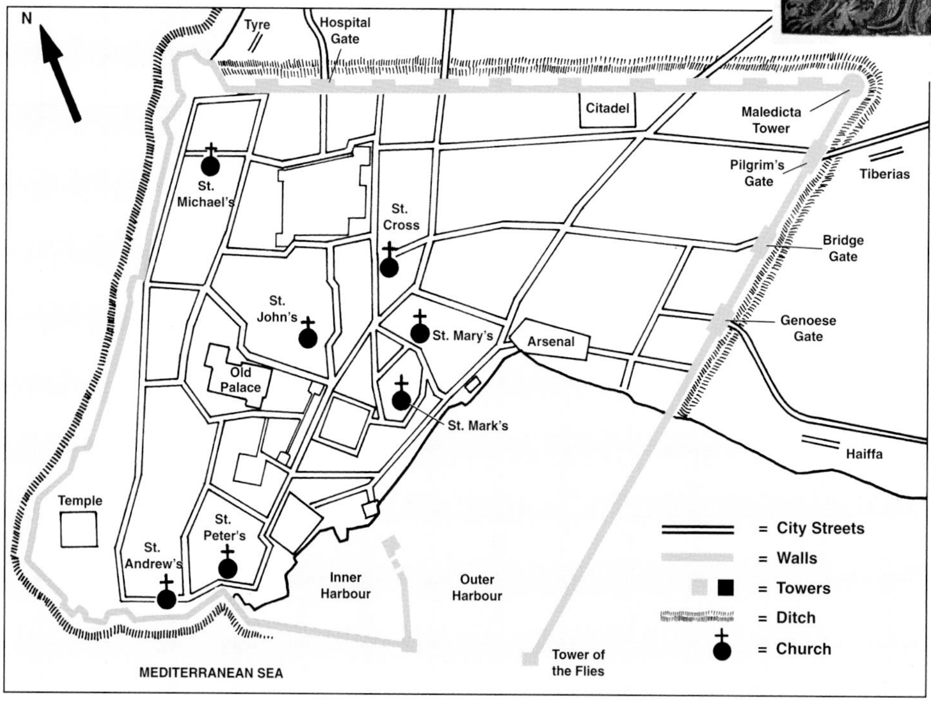

LEFT: *Acre, the greatest city on the coast of the Holy Land, at the time of the siege. It had very strong defences and, as Guy was to discover, a strong, determined and well-led garrison.*

Map labels: N, Tyre, Hospital Gate, Citadel, Maledicta Tower, Pilgrim's Gate, Tiberias, St. Michael's, St. Cross, Bridge Gate, St. John's, St. Mary's, Arsenal, Genoese Gate, Old Palace, St. Mark's, Haiffa, Temple, St. Peter's, St. Andrew's, Inner Harbour, Outer Harbour, Tower of the Flies, MEDITERRANEAN SEA

= City Streets
= Walls
= Towers
= Ditch
= Church

protected by high walls. Acre was thus a valuable prize and its strong defences meant that it was very difficult to take. Indeed, it was a model of the problems and techniques of siege warfare.

SALADIN'S RUN OF VICTORIES

Following his victory at Hattin, Saladin enjoyed a series of successes against the crusaders, and between July and September 1187 he took major cities such as Tiberias and Ascalon. He also took Acre, which fell after only a token siege in July 1187. Saladin imposed the most generous terms on the garrison and inhabitants. He also installed his best engineer, Karakush, as the new commander, with instructions to bring the defences up to the highest state of readiness.

Saladin also invested the city of Tyre but without immediate success, being thwarted at the last minute by the chance arrival of a small group of Christian reinforcements from Byzantium. This group was led by a very energetic and ambitious Italian nobleman, Conrad of Montferrat, who quickly rallied the garrison, which had been on the verge of surrender. Conrad was quickly elected the leader of the defences, and shortly afterwards Saladin left to attack what both sides recognised as the ultimate prize – Jerusalem – launching his attack on

ABOVE: Siege towers were formidable, but they were vulnerable to various forms of attack. In particular, being made of wood, they could be destroyed by fire, as happened several times during the Siege of Acre.

September 20, 1187.

The Christian garrison at Jerusalem surrendered after only two weeks' resistance, but Saladin's terms were again very generous: some Christians were ransomed and a number were sent into captivity, but the others were allowed to leave. With Jerusalem in his hands, Saladin returned to Tyre, but his army was growing restive at the length of the campaign and after several abortive attempts to take the fortress the saracen leader abandoned the operation on December 31,1187.

KING GUY OF JERUSALEM

One of the crusaders who had been captured by Saladin at the Battle of Hattin was King Guy of Jerusalem. The Christian monarch was held a prisoner until he swore on oath that he would never again take up arms against the Muslims. On the strength of that oath, Saladin released his enemy in April 1189, but Guy wasted no time in finding a priest who was prepared to inform him that such an oath to an "infidel" could not be considered binding on a Christian prince.

With his conscience salved, Guy declared that he was free to take up arms once again and set about recovering his kingdom. His first step was to establish a temporary capital, which he would use until he had regained Jerusalem. His first choice was Tyre, but he met an immediate rebuff when, in late April 1189, he tried to enter that city, where the arrogant Conrad felt so secure that he would not even allow the king through the city gates. Infuriated, Guy laid siege to Tyre, even though it was a very strong fortress and had successfully withstood two attacks by Saladin.

Meanwhile, news of the disaster at Hattin and of the loss of Jerusalem and other cities had reached Europe, and Christian reinforcements were beginning to arrive to wrest the Holy Land back from Saladin and his armies. Among the first to reach Tyre were two Italian contingents from Genoa and Pisa, which brought siege engines with them. These were greeted rudely by Conrad but most effusively by Guy. Not surprisingly, the Italians threw in their lot with the latter. But, instead of employing them against Tyre, Guy decided to pursue a much more audacious goal and, in August 1189, in one of the most extraordinary decisions in military history, he took his weak, ill-equipped and poorly organised army, consisting of approximately 600 knights and 7,000 infantry, southwards to lay siege to the mighty Muslim stronghold at Acre.

On arrival on August 28 Guy established a camp on the hill at Toron, some three-quarters of a mile (1.2km) outside the city walls. On August 31 he launched a quick attack in an over-optimistic attempt to take the defenders by surprise. It failed and Guy realised that he would be in for a long siege but, apparently undaunted, he started to fortify his camp. For once, however, fortune proved to be with King Guy. His siege of the Muslim stronghold proved to be an effective rallying cry for the Christians such that a steady stream of reinforcements began to arrive from Europe and from elsewhere in the Holy Land, starting in September with groups of Danish, Flemish, French and Frisian knights and their supporters.

Saladin was initially taken by surprise, partly because yet another crusader had gone back on a solemn promise, but also because the prospect of such a small and ill-equipped army overcoming the well-fortified garrison at Acre seemed so far-fetched. Nevertheless, he arrived in mid-September with a saracen army and set up an armed camp a short distance inland from the crusaders, thus sandwiching Guy's army between his force and the city walls.

In two hastily mounted operations Saladin sent a resupply column into the city and also drove the crusaders off a small hill that they had taken in order to dominate the road northwards to Tyre. The crusaders did, however, retain a stretch of shoreline, which meant that reinforcements and supplies could be delivered over the beach.

RIGHT: Two forms of battering ram, one carried on men's shoulders, the other suspended from a frame.

SALADIN (1138-1193)

The saracen leader known in the west as Saladin was a man of great integrity who was respected by the crusaders almost as much as by the saracens. His correct Arab name was Salah ad-Din Yusuf and he was born at Tikr´yt (in modern-day Iraq) in 1138, a member of the Kurdish Ayyubid family.

In 1152, aged fourteen, he enlisted in the army of the Syrian ruler, Nûr ad-Dîn and his natural abilities as a soldier brought him a meteoric rise. Between 1164 and 1169 he took part in the three Syrian expeditions that were sent to Egypt to help the Egyptian rulers, the Fatimids, to repel attacks by the Palestine-based crusaders.

Saladin so distinguished himself that in 1169, the ruler, Zur ad-Din, appointed him commander of the Syrian army and vizier of Egypt. In this post Saladin was nominally subject to the authority of the Fatimid caliph in Cairo, but he exerted a wide-ranging authority, revitalising Egypt's economy and reorganising its army and navy.

After Zur ad-Din's death in 1174, Saladin determined to expel the crusaders, but first he took steps to secure his own his power base in Syria and northern Mesopotamia, taking Damascus in 1174, Aleppo in 1183 and Mosul in 1186. He was then ready to challenge the crusaders and in 1187 he invaded the crusader kingdom of Jerusalem, his first notable victory being at the Battle of Hattin on July 4, 1187, where he totally defeated the forces led by King Guy. Saladin then captured Jerusalem in October 1187 and would probably have gone on to expel the crusaders from the Holy Land had it not been for one man, with whom Saladin's name is for ever linked, King Richard I of England.

THE THIRD CRUSADE

Unfortunately for him, Saladin's victories in 1187 sparked off the Third Crusade, whose primary aim was to win back the Holy City. Saladin made strenuous military efforts to defeat the new wave of crusaders, but the newly arrived Richard foiled the saracen efforts to break the siege of Acre, which fell in 1191. The crusaders, led by Richard, then advanced towards Jerusalem but Saladin's scorched earth policy left them with no choice but to withdraw to the coast, even though they were in sight of their goal. In 1192 Saladin was again foiled by Richard at Jaffa, and the two men concluded an armistice agreement under which the crusaders retained a strip of coastal territory but left Jerusalem in Muslim hands, albeit with a guaranteed right of access by Christian pilgrims. Unfortunately for historians, the two men never actually met, even though in several battles they can have been no more than a few hundred yards apart and within sight of each other.

Following the agreement with Saladin, Richard left for England in 1192 and the great saracen general died in Damascus on March 4 the following year, after the briefest of illnesses.

AN HONOURABLE MAN

There are many stories suppporting Saladin's reputation for honour, integrity, generosity and magnanimity, although it is sometimes difficult to separate fact from fantasy. It is, however, well documented that he often prevented his own men from massacring crusaders, even though there had been many examples of crusaders wantonly killing saracens. One incident widely accepted as true is said to have occurred at the siege of

THE BATTLE OF OCTOBER 4, 1187

Guy knew that he would be able to concentrate on the siege only if he could resolve the problem of the threat from Saladin at his rear. His first attempt to achieve this was made on October 4 in a battle in which the balance swung backwards and forwards several times in the course of a bitterly fought day. From the moment he arrived Saladin knew that he would be attacked by the crusaders but, even so, when it came, the crusaders managed to take him completely by surprise. The crusaders emerged from their camp just after dawn with the Templars in the van and King Guy in the centre accompanied by four knights carrying a silk cushion bearing the symbol of the Gospel. This was being used as a substitute for the relic of the True Cross, which, of course, had been lost to the Saracens at Hattin.

Acre where a distraught crusader woman was found near their camp by saracen soldiers, wailing that a saracen had grabbed her baby girl and made off with her. She was brought before Saladin who promptly ordered a search of his camp, and as soon as the child was found she was restored to her mother and they were both safely passed back to the crusader camp. Another story concerns the Battle of Jaffa, where Richard the Lionheart was constantly in the midst of the fighting. Apparently, when Saladin saw Richard knocked to the ground and in mortal danger, the saracen chief sent him a new horse in order that the fight could be continued on a fair basis.

A WORTHY EXCHANGE

When Richard the Lionheart was about to return to England in 1192 he sent a message to Saladin, informing the saracen leader of his departure, but adding that it was only temporary and that he would return in three years' time to gain complete control of the Holy Land. Saladin immediately replied that if it became inevitable that he should lose, then there was no prince to whom he would rather do so than Richard. It was an elegant and worthy exchange between two great gentlemen.

RIGHT: A portrait of Saladin, from a Persian manuscript, ca. 1180. He was both a great general and an exceptionally gifted man, not averse to showing mercy in a cruel age.

Gerard of Ridefort, commanding the Knights Templar, opened the proceedings with an attack on the Saracen right wing, which was commanded by Saladin's nephew, Taqi al-Din. Taqi decided to entrap the crusaders by feigning flight, a ruse which he thought would cause the crusader column to become extended. Following this, choosing his moment, Taqi would order his men to turn and attack. It was an audacious plan, but unfortunately for the saracens Taqi failed to inform his uncle of this plan, so that when the army commander saw his right wing in apparent flight he misunderstood the situation and immediately despatched reinforcements from the centre. This precipitate reaction caused severe problems, since it seriously disrupted the saracen centre without doing much to help the right wing.

Seeing the confusion in the saracen ranks the crusaders seized their opportunity and King Guy led a charge against the Muslim centre, which severely rattled the saracen troops, who gave way, with a number fleeing in disorder. As usually happened with cavalry charges, however, the momentum of their successful charge carried the crusader knights some distance before their commanders could bring them under control, turn them around and lead them back to the battle.

There then occurred a series of comparatively trivial and totally unpredictable events, which resulted in the advantage swinging rapidly and arbitrarily between the two sides. The first of these occurred when the servants in the saracen camp saw Taqi's knights riding to the rear pursued by crusaders. Thinking (as did Saladin) that the saracen knights were actually in flight, the servants leapt to the conclusion that all was lost. Knowing from previous experience that they would receive scant mercy from the crusaders, the camp servants panicked, grabbed what booty they could from their masters' tents, and set out eastwards as fast as they could go.

ABOVE: *The Holy Roman Emperor, Frederick Barbarossa, with his court. He was a great leader and led a large army across Europe, only to be drowned when only a few hundred miles from Jerusalem.*

Then, exactly as the servants had feared, the returning crusader knights came across the almost empty saracen camp, and killed the few remaining guards and servants. The crusaders then settled down to some serious looting, which was always a prime consideration among them as they sought to defray the great personal expense of taking part in the crusade. So involved did they become that, through some extraordinary oversight, none of them cut down Saladin's tent, which would have been taken as a signal that the entire saracen army had been defeated and could well have led to a great crusader victory.

Nevertheless, the crusaders were clearly winning, when the second of these trivial and totally unpredictable events occurred. As the crusader knights pillaged the saracen camp a horse threw its rider, a German knight. As frightened horses tend to do, it galloped away, by chance in the direction of the crusader lines, leaving its rider stranded. At this, some foot soldiers ran after the horse to catch it and return it to its owner. But other crusaders, espying a riderless, galloping horse hotly pursued by shouting, running men, assumed them to be fleeing from an advancing enemy and, taking alarm, began to follow them in ever increasing numbers.

Meanwhile, Saladin had brought his own men under control and, seeing the crusaders starting to withdraw towards their own lines, he led a charge into their rear, turning a disorderly withdrawal into a rout, in which many hundreds of crusaders were killed. Total victory was now within Saladin's grasp, but at this point he was surrounded by his own knights who were furious that their property had been looted by their own servants, who were now leaving the battlefield in large numbers. Accordingly, they forced Saladin to turn his attention from finishing off the crusaders in order to despatch a group of cavalry to catch the thieves and to bring them and their booty back to the camp.

By the end of this eventful day a large number of crusaders and a lesser number of saracens had been killed, but strategically the situation had not changed at all. The Muslim garrison inside the walls was still besieged, Saladin's army had not broken the siege, and Guy's crusader army was still intact, but still sandwiched between two groups of saracens.

THE SIEGE CONTINUES

As tended to happen in medieval sieges, matters now settled into something of a routine. The crusaders managed to complete a massive trench around the landward side of the fortress, designed to prevent forays by the garrison, while their ships sought to impose a naval blockade. They also built earth walls around their camp in order to protect it from attacks from the rear by Saladin. Within the city, the saracen garrison was on short commons, but all was by no means lost. Swimmers managed to carry messages in and out of the fortress and occasional supply ships managed to break through to bring in much needed supplies. The crusaders carried out periodic assaults, and the defenders beat drums and fired flares to alert Saladin, who then attacked the crusaders in their rear.

The crusaders were totally cut off by land by Saladin's army outside their lines, but since their right flank rested on the sea they were able to maintain communications with the outside world. Thus, they were able to receive both supplies and reinforcements, either directly from Europe or from their supply base at Tyre. The numbers of men and horses increased out of proportion to the food and fodder available – all of which now had to be brought in by sea – and, as a result, the crusaders began to suffer from hunger and disease. Saladin, however, was not without problems of his own, since his army was being reduced by men returning home, and he was left with insufficient numbers to carry out a serious attack on the crusader camp.

The siege continued throughout the winter of 1189-90 with the crusaders concentrating on building three immense siege towers. Then in March 1190 Conrad of Montferrat, temporarily reconciled to King Guy, brought a relief convoy from Tyre and managed to avoid contact with the patrolling saracen galleys that were seeking to prevent much-needed supplies and reinforcements from reaching the crusaders.

The crusaders cleared three approaches to the fortress walls, and at the end of April the siege towers were moved until they were close up against the walls. All three towers were some 100ft (31m) high, so that the archers on the top floor were able to fire down into the city, causing much mayhem among the defenders. The saracens tried desperately to destroy the towers using naphtha but failed and then made a tentative offer to surrender, but their terms were refused by the crusaders. At this, a renewed attack was made on the siege towers, led by an engineer who devised a new form of fire attack, as a result of which one tower was destroyed in flames, killing all those inside. On seeing this, the occupants of the other siege towers fled in panic and the saracens sortied from the nearest gates to destroy these towers as well.

BELOW: *The triumphal entry of King Philip Augustus of France (left) and King Richard I of England (but not, it should be noted, King Guy of Jerusalem), led by saracen officials (bottom right) bearing the city's keys.*

In May 1190 Saladin, having received some reinforcements, carried out a series of attacks on the crusaders over an eight-day period, but by this time the latter had improved the defences of their camp with ditches and walls, and they managed to survive. Then, in late July, it was the crusaders' turn to attack Saladin, but they too were repulsed with heavy casualties.

A few days after this attack, on July 27, the crusaders received unexpected reinforcements in the shape of a large French contingent under the command of Count Henry of Champagne. Henry was the nephew of both the Kings of England and France and thus, despite the apparent disparity in their titles, he was considered senior to King Guy of Jerusalem and assumed command of the crusader force.

Meanwhile, the crusaders had turned their attention to a ram, which had been constructed throughout the summer, using the mainmast of one of the many ships stuck on the beach. It had a roof and was covered in animal skins that had been soaked in vinegar, which was supposed to make them fire resistant. When the ram was put into use in October, however, the fort's defenders managed to destroy it by fire, as they had the towers previously.

The crusaders did not limit their attacks to the land, and in September two very imaginative naval assaults were carried out. In one a siege tower was constructed on a platform, which rested upon two galleys lashed together by ropes. This was then used to attack the Tower of Flies, which stood at the end of the southern mole. But, as had happened elsewhere, the defenders managed to set fire to the floating tower and it was destroyed. Then the crusaders tried to use fire themselves, this time by sending a fireship into Acre harbour, but, although there were many saracen ships in the harbour, little damage was done. Nevertheless, this was a remarkable operation and was one of the first – if not the first – recorded uses of such a tactic, which was to become quite common down to the 19th Century.

CONDITIONS IN THE CRUSADER CAMP

As described earlier, the crusader camp was sandwiched between the fortress and the saracen camp, and conditions within it deteriorated rapidly. Hygiene was very poor and the campsite was filthy in the extreme, resulting in a great deal of sickness, mainly dysentery, and a variety of diseases including typhus and scurvy. Indeed, over the entire period of the siege, more crusaders died from sickness than in military action. To add to the crusaders' problems there was rampant inflation and food was both very scarce and extremely expensive.

On October 4 the survivors of the German crusade arrived, but since their emperor,

KING RICHARD I OF ENGLAND

There are some people whose deeds are written indelibly on the pages of history and mention of whose name conjures up an instant picture of a person and a time. One member of that select band is King Richard I, known in England as "The Lionheart", in France as "Coeur de Lion" and in Germany as "Löwenherz".

Richard was born on September 8, 1157, at Beaumont Palace in the English university town of Oxford. He was one of eight children of two remarkable parents. His father was a Plantagenet, King Henry II of England (1133-1189), while his mother was Eleanor, Queen of England and Duchess of Aquitaine (1122-1204). Henry II, who reigned from 1154 to 1189, was a great administrative reformer, who resolved many territorial and judicial disputes in the British Isles, although he is best remembered for his quarrel with Thomas O'Becket, Archbishop of Canterbury.

When she married Henry in 1152, Eleanor retained her

duchy of Aquitaine. Richard, who was much closer to his mother than to his father, spent much of his youth at her court in Poitiers. In 1172, Eleanor insisted that Richard, then aged 15, should be made Duke of Aquitaine, and he then became involved in several military campaigns, some of them against his father. It was during this period that he attended a tournament held by King Sancho VI of Navarre, where the king's daughter, Berengaria (1163-1230), set eyes on the dashing, handsome young prince, fell in love and resolved to marry him.

In 1187 the death of his elder brother meant that Richard became heir to the throne of England and just two years later his father died and the young prince became King Richard the First. Shortly afterwards, Richard set out on the Third Crusade to honour a vow made by his father, leaving his mother, Queen Eleanor, as regent. He met King Philip II of France and they set out together, although they did not get on at all well. One particular cause of dispute was that Richard had been betrothed to Philip's sister since they were both infants and while they were in Sicily en route to the Holy Land Richard announced that he would not marry her but Berengaria of Navarre. Soon after, Queen Eleanor went to Navarre, collected Berengaria, and took her to Sicily, although Richard did not marry the princess immediately and she was placed in the care of Richard's beloved sister, Joanna, whose husband, King William II of Sicily, had recently died.

Joanna and Berengaria set out for the Holy Land, but their ship was diverted by a storm and was wrecked on Cyprus, where, despite their royal status, they were treated very badly by the ruler, Isaac Comnenus. Richard then arrived and without having intended to do so, became involved in a war with the ruler, whom he defeated in a short, sharp campaign. Richard then married Berengaria in Limassol in1191

Frederick Barbarossa, had drowned in Anatolia, they were now under the command of his son, Friedrich von Schwaben, a much less effective leader. However, they did bring with them a siege engine and a very large battering ram. A few days later the advance guard of the English crusaders arrived, together with Baldwin, the Archbishop of Canterbury. It is also reported that another form of reinforcement arrived in October, in the shape of 300 ladies of "easy virtue" offering a different type of solace to the weary crusaders.

Meanwhile, the siege operations continued. The newly arrived Germans carried out an unsuccessful assault in November, and by mid-December the saracen garrison inside Acre was on the verge of starvation and began another round of negotiations for a surrender. Once again, Saladin managed to stave off defeat by sending a large force of twenty-five ships, which fought their way through the crusader blockade and averted the crisis inside the fortress.

The winter of 1190-91 was both bleak and very wet, and the unusually heavy rains so undermined the walls of the fortress that a part fell down, taking both defenders and besiegers by surprise. The crusaders managed to organise themselves and attempted to

BELOW LEFT: Richard I fighting in the Holy Land. There can be no doubt that he was very brave, always leading from the front and in the thick of the fighting.

RIGHT: Richard I, King of England. One of England's greatest and most loved heroes, his courage and example counted for more than the heavy taxes he imposed.

and set out for the Holy Land. Immediately he arrived at Acre he became involved in the siege. Joan and Berengaria then arrived and watched Richard bring the long drawn-out siege to a successful conclusion.

Richard then led the crusaders down the coast and inland towards Jerusalem, although he was unable actually to reach the Holy City. Repeated disagreements with Philip led to the French king returning home, leaving Richard who eventually made a truce with Saladin, under which the saracens held onto Jerusalem, while the crusaders retained a strip along the coast. Saladin also personally guaranteed the safety of Christian pilgrims visiting the various shrines.

Berengaria then set out for Aquitaine to await Richard's arrival, while her husband set out separately for England. However, while en route he was captured by Duke Leopold V of Austria, who claimed that he had been insulted by Richard in the aftermath of the siege of Acre. A large ransom was set for Richard's release, and this was collected with great efficiency by the redoubtable Eleanor in England and Berengaria in Aquitaine. Richard finally made it home to England, where he found that his younger brother, John, supported by Philip of France, had been conspiring against him. Richard sorted things out in England, was crowned and then left almost immediately for France, where he was reunited with Berengaria and fought a series of campaigns against Philip.

Richard was taking part in a very minor skirmish in 1199 when he was wounded by an arrow. The wound festered and

Richard died, having forgiven the man who had shot him. Richard's courtiers were so furious at the death of their beloved king that, despite Richard's forgiveness, they found the man who had shot the fatal arrow, and killed him. Berengaria was present at Richard's side as he died; she never remarried and devoted the rest of her life to charitable works. Berengaria was the only known queen of England never to have set foot in England.

Richard was one of the most courageous warriors of his age. Under his rule his kingdom was heavily taxed to support his campaigns and to pay for his ransom from Austria. His dash and daring, and the magic that surrounded his deeds, were, however, such that his subjects forgave him and he became one of the greatest and most loved heroes of English history.

carry out an assault, but they were so hampered by the continuing rain that they failed, and after a struggle the saracens managed to repair the breach. By now all involved were suffering intensely, although Saladin managed to get another convoy into Acre in February, while the crusaders were saved by a convoy which arrived in March. The sickness in the crusader camp continued, claiming Friedrich von Schwaben in January, leaving the German contingent leaderless until Leopold of Austria arrived in April.

While these events were taking place, two kings, Philip II of France and Richard I of England, each accompanied by a large group of knights, had been making their way by land and sea towards the Holy Land. They had started out together, but split up, with Philip and the French contingent arriving at Acre on April 20, where they immediately threw themselves into the battle. Richard and the main body of the English, however, were driven by storms, first to Rhodes and later to Cyprus, eventually reaching Acre some two months later. When they did arrive, however, they did so in spectacular fashion, catching and disposing of a large saracen supply ship carrying 700 troops, following which Richard and his men landed on the beach beside the crusader camp on June 12, 1191.

Once Richard came ashore the crusaders had another command crisis. One faction under Philip consisted of the French and the Genoese, the other of Richard, supported by King Guy and the Pisan contingent. Richard, however, was in a much better financial position and was able to attract many uncommitted knights to his banner by offering them more pay than Philip could manage. Thus, Richard took command of the siege and startled everyone by offering to meet Saladin face to face, although the latter refused on the grounds that commanders did not meet until the terms had been agreed. Saladin did, however, send his brother Safadin to meet Richard and these two spent three days in discussions, but apparently without reaching any significant agreement.

ABOVE: One of the most controversial of Richard's acts was the killing of some 2,700 saracen prisoners taken at the fall of Acre, which took place outside the city walls on August 20, 1191.

Richard now suffered from his first bout of the local sickness and while he was *hors de combat* an attack on Acre was led by Philip. For a variety of reasons, this turned out to be an expensive failure. First, many of Philip's soldiers, particularly the mercenaries, including, critically, the engineers, had transferred their loyalties to Richard and did not take part in the attack. Second, Saladin carried out a diversionary raid on the eastern end of the crusader trenches, which enabled the garrison inside Acre first to repulse Philip's attack and then to venture outside the walls to destroy many of the French siege engines.

RICHARD IN COMMAND

Richard proved to be a highly capable military commander, with a special aptitude for siege warfare. Thus, throughout this period the siege engines continued battering, while sappers were digging away at the walls. Several targets were under attack, but Richard's main concern was with the Maledicta tower, which came under almost continuous bombardment.

Richard also devised a system of employing his men in alternating infantry assaults and engineering work. By ringing the changes, he kept them relatively fresh. Determined to bring matters to a successful conclusion, Richard also had an increasing number of siege towers brought into action and moved close to the walls from where their archers could make life very difficult for the defenders. The great majority of these siege engines were built and operated by the different national contingents, but one was paid for by donations from individual crusaders and operated by an international crew. It was known as "God's Own Catapult" and, perhaps because of this auspicious name, was successful in shattering one of Acre's strongest walls.

THE FINAL STAGES

On July 2, a section of the wall near the Maledicta tower collapsed and the following day the French assaulted the breach but were driven back. On the same day the saracen general, Taqi, tried to lead a relief force into Acre, but was also beaten back.

On the night of July 5, mining under the Maledicta tower resulted in a further collapse. A furious battle quickly developed as the crusaders sought to consolidate their gains by getting rid of the debris (which was in the way of an assault) with Richard offering huge sums to soldiers to carry it away. Although the crusaders suffered heavy losses, this was partially achieved and the French put in a second assault on July 7. This was followed by a further attack by Richard on July 11, with a force made up of English and Pisans. All these assaults were, however, repulsed due to the difficulties of getting through the rubble.

Saladin was aware that matters were reaching a climax and attacked the crusaders from outside, but was beaten off, and the saracen garrison realised that nothing more would be achieved by holding out. So, on July 12, the city commander offered terms, his first proposal including giving up Acre free and clear, returning the fragment of the Holy Cross to the crusaders together with 200 Christian captives held in the city, and handing over 50 of his own men as hostages. As was normal in such negotiations, this first offer was rejected out of hand, so the saracens came up with a second proposal, which, in addition to the city and the Holy Cross, included the return of 2,000 noble Christians and the handing over of 500 saracen prisoners. Also, the saracen garrison would abandon the city, each man taking just his clothing, with all weapons, food and other property being left in Acre. The saracens also offered 200,000 saracen talents, to be given personally to King Richard and King Philip, and a further 40,000 to Conrad of Montferrat, who had negotiated the surrender (but none, it should be noted for King Guy), together with some valuable saracen nobles as hostages against good faith. A significant feature of this offer was that the great majority of the returned Christian prisoners and the money would have to come from outside the city, but Saladin was not consulted as to whether he could meet such terms. Despite this, the terms were agreed and the hostages were duly delivered to the crusaders on Friday July 12, with the settlement of the balance due to take place on August 20.

THE MASSACRE

Thus the long siege, so rashly initiated by King Guy many months earlier, ended in a crusader triumph, but any description of the fall of Acre would be incomplete without mention of the tragic sequel. Despite having been neither consulted nor a signatory to the agreement, Saladin was a man of impeccable honour and considered himself duty bound to comply with its terms. In essence, this meant that he had to assemble a large number of captured crusaders, many of them by name, who were being held prisoner in various places throughout the saracen lands, to raise the very considerable sum of money involved, again from various sources, and to achieve both by August 20.

Saladin did his best, but was defeated by two factors – time and distance. Just before the deadline he informed Richard's emissaries that he needed more time, but that he would immediately release such prisoners as had arrived and hand over the money he had by then accumulated. According to the customs of the period, this would have meant that the crusaders would have remained in possession of some 3,000 saracen prisoners until Saladin could meet the terms in full. But Richard desperately wanted to move onto the next stage in his campaign, which was to take the port of Jaffa as a necessary preliminary to striking inland at the ultimate goal of Jerusalem. He could not, however, achieve this if he had to guard and feed all the prisoners. Therefore, Saladin having failed to meet the conditions, Richard ordered that every saracen man, woman and child held by the crusaders as a result of taking Acre – some 2,700 in all – was to be killed. This was carried out in a bloody and violent slaughter on the afternoon of August 20.

Over the succeeding centuries this has been condemned as an atrocious act. It was, however, by no means unique: there were many other examples of mass slaughter of prisoners. For instance, when the crusaders captured Jerusalem in 1099, they had murdered every last inhabitant, while twelve years earlier Saladin had ordered the execution of every Templar captured at the Battle of Hattin, a total of some 300. Somewhat later, in the 1370s, the famous and greatly admired French knight, du Guesclin, on two separate occasions captured large numbers of English prisoners. When bitter wrangling arose within his own ranks as to whom the prisoners belonged (and thus who would gain the ransoms) he ended the quarrelling by killing the lot.

Chapter 7

THE BATTLE OF JAFFA

Once Richard had decided that it would be more than usually foolhardy to continue operations against Jerusalem he withdrew the bulk of the crusader army, first to the coast and then to Acre, which he reached on July 22, 1192. With his army and fleet intact, Richard was determined to hold the coastal strip and was getting ready to besiege Beirut, the one port still held by the saracens, when he heard that Saladin had attacked the crusader garrison at the fortified port of Jaffa (modern-day Tel Aviv).

For his part, Saladin had heard that Richard was at Acre and, assuming that the English king was preparing to leave the Holy Land, he decided to capture Jaffa while Richard's attention was focused elsewhere. As a result, the crusader garrison in Jaffa was taken by surprise when the saracen army appeared on July 26. The commander just had time to despatch a messenger to Richard warning him of the impending attack before closing the gates and preparing to resist the inevitable siege. Saladin launched the first assault against the outer walls on the following day, and after only four days the saracen attackers broke through, driving the defending crusaders back into the citadel.

As often happened in sieges, as soon as the saracen troops gained entry to the town they became carried away by their success and set to looting the town, ignoring their leaders' order to attack the citadel. Nevertheless, Saladin invited the garrison to surrender, which they agreed to do, provided that they had not been rescued by three o'clock the following afternoon, a somewhat strange request but one to which Saladin readily agreed.

RICHARD SAILS TO THE RESCUE
Richard, meanwhile, had received the garrison commander's message and, with his usual energy, rapidly mobilised a rescue force to which the French, for reasons of their own, refused to contribute. Richard wasted no time in trying to persuade his recalcitrant "allies" and set out for Jaffa, which was some 50 miles (80km) to the south. As he frequently did in such coastal operations, Richard split his force into two, with most of the mounted knights travelling in a group along the coast road, while he and a small force of knights and foot soldiers sailed in seven galleys. The naval force was delayed and split up by the winds, so that the first element to arrive off Jaffa consisted of just three ships. It is not difficult to imagine the pressure the impatient king placed upon the unfortunate captain of his own ship and it is, therefore, no surprise that his was one of those three.

As his ship approached the shore, Richard had some difficulty in establishing what was happening and all he could see at first was the citadel surrounded by throngs of saracen troops. All became clear, however, when a daring priest jumped off the battlements and swam out to the royal galley to give the king an account of what was happening. Ashore, Saladin had been warned that a Christian rescue force was on its way, but he seems to have underestimated Richard's speed of reaction and was taken by surprise when he was suddenly told that Richard was aboard one of the ships standing off the castle and was about to disembark. The saracen commander immediately ordered his men to take the citadel at once. The 50 remaining crusaders in the citadel agreed to surrender, but carried on playing for time, using whatever delaying tactics were available to them to give Richard the opportunity to come to their rescue.

RIGHT: Thirsting for the fray, Richard I arrived off besieged Jaffa and was so impatient that he leapt into the water, followed by some 80 knights, taking the saracens completely by surprise. Indeed, without this impetuous action the citadel would undoubtedly have fallen within an hour or so.

Aboard his ship, Richard was so impatient that he was not fully dressed for battle, but despite this he grabbed his sword and leapt into the sea, which, fortunately for him, was only waist-deep. The king started for the shore followed by 80 knights and some foot soldiers. Even some of the ship's crew were inspired by the excitement to join them. Such was the rush, however, that there was time to disembark only three horses.

Meanwhile, most of the saracen leaders were involved in the taking of the citadel and were out of sight on the other side of the castle, involving themselves in the formalities of surrender. The surviving crusaders were in the process of handing themselves over to the saracens, while the Patriarch of Jerusalem was in Saladin's tent, also surrendering himself. On the shore, however, the massed saracen troops saw Richard's crusaders wading through the shallows. Since one of the ships was the royal red, they knew that Richard must be among them, and such was his reputation for ferocity in battle that he and his handful of men soon put the saracens to flight.

Richard led his men, by now supported by those from the other four galleys which had just arrived, to the citadel gate, where they erected a temporary palisade from the jetsam lying on the beach. Having consolidated their position and caught their breath, the crusaders then broke into the city and stormed into the citadel, where they kicked out the remaining few looters, grabbed one of the only three surviving horses from the stables and chased the fleeing saracens. Outside the city, news of the arrival of the dreaded English king spread quickly and the saracen army fled, even though it greatly outnumbered Richard's force, carrying Saladin with it.

THE SARACEN COUNTER-ATTACK

By the time Saladin brought his panicking soldiers to a halt they were some miles away. Later in the day, having stabilised the situation, he sent a delegation to Richard in an effort to work out terms for a truce. Both leaders wanted peace, albeit for different motives, but the negotiations ground to a halt over just one issue, the future of the fortified port of Ascalon, which, for different but vital reasons, both Richard and Saladin wanted.

With the negotiations temporarily suspended, Richard returned to working on the fortifications – he was never too mighty to shirk physical labour alongside his men when the situation demanded it – and nightfall found him still at work outside the walls. Rather than go

into the citadel, he simply made camp where he was, protected by just a few men who had been working with him. The saracens had been keeping him under observation and, seeing that he had placed himself in a very vulnerable position, they made a hasty plan to capture him in a surprise attack. The raiding party (a "snatch squad" in modern parlance) was moving quietly into position, when, very fortunately for Richard, one of his knights heard them and managed to wake the king and his companions. Instantly alert, the royal party just had time to don their mail vests over their nightshirts before leaping onto their horses and escaping into the darkness.

This attempt to capture Richard was, in fact, just one part of a concerted saracen attack on Jaffa and the other element managed to force its way into the city, leaving Richard cut off outside. Thus, as confused fighting broke out, Richard was once again in the thick of things and was forced to produce a new plan in response to the sudden emergency, a combination of circumstances which always brought out the best in him.

Once again Richard set up a temporary palisade, using empty barrels, driftwood and any other materials immediately to hand, which gave him a brief respite in which to reorganise his men. Then, leaving one group on the palisade, he and some 60-odd knights charged into Jaffa, where they managed to force out the astonished saracens.

THE FINAL BATTLE

Neither side was prepared to concede defeat. King Richard then reorganised the garrison for another defensive action, his chosen battleground being a piece of flat ground outside the city walls at the temporary palisade. At this stage Richard had some 2,000 men, of whom 400 were crossbowmen and, even in this extremity, he was prepared to devise new and devastatingly effective tactics, setting out his infantry in three ranks. In the front rank were pikemen, who knelt, holding their pikes at an angle of about 45 degrees and with their bases stuck in the sand, providing a virtually impenetrable obstacle to the saracen cavalry. Between each pair of pikemen and slightly to their rear stood a crossbowman, his weapon at the ready. Behind him stood at least one man whose job was to reload the spare crossbows and pass them forward to the firer. This arrangement resulted in a steady volume of high velocity, aimed fire, devastating against either cavalry or infantry who ventured into range. The mounted crusader knights, of whom not too many remained by this stage in the battle, were formed into a counter-attack force, which charged any isolated group of saracen cavalry.

The battle was fought for several hours, during which the crusaders' discipline held firm, although this may have been prompted Richard's threat that he would personally behead anyone who left the line. After several hours of heavy fighting – with Richard always in the thick of it – saracen losses became such that their morale collapsed and the point was eventually reached where they refused Saladin's orders to charge yet again.

Thus the battle ended. It was, in many ways, a crusader victory but, in fact, the two sides were completely exhausted and after some posturing both Richard and Saladin were only too pleased to sign a three-year truce. Saladin still demanded Ascalon, and still Richard refused to hand it over. In the end they reached a masterly compromise and agreed to demolish it, which was carried out by joint crusader/saracen working parties. Saladin also allowed any crusader who wished to do so to carry out his or her personal pilgrimage to Jerusalem, and guaranteed their safety, an undertaking which was rigidly enforced.

TWO GREAT WARRIORS

The pace of events in this most memorable of battles was breathtaking as Richard repeatedly just managed to stave off defeat. His personal contribution was exceptional: he was always at the point of greatest threat, always in the thick of the fighting, and always in imminent danger of being either killed or captured, but he always managed to escape by the skin of his teeth. But Richard was not just a "mighty warrior": as the Battle of Jaffa so clearly showed, he had a brilliant grasp of tactics and repeatedly deployed his very limited resources to maximum effect.

It would appear at first sight that Saladin and the saracens had not done particularly well. However, the saracen army was simply exhausted, having been fighting and marching continuously for many months. Like Richard's, Saladin's army was made up of various contingents with varying degrees of autonomy, and the commander had to cajole them as much as command them. Then, despite the excellence of their own commander, the individual saracens appear to have become overawed, not only by Richard's reputation, but also by his actual performance.

LEFT: An allegorical painting of Richard and Saladin in hand-to-hand combat. In reality the two men never met, although they were several times within several hundred yards of each other.

Chapter 8

THE RESULTS OF THE CRUSADES

In many ways the crusades were a splendid achievement. In those unsophisticated, medieval times the countries of central, northern and western Europe, who were almost always at war with each other, managed to agree on a goal and to work together for what was perceived to be the common good. There had, of course, been alliances before, but they had tended to be temporary, and the crusades were the first occasion in which such a large group of nations agreed to work together and succeeded in doing so over such a lengthy period.

The crusaders managed to move large groups of people by land and sea over the long distances that lay between their home countries and the Holy Land. The groups involved consisted not just of knights and foot soldiers, but also of priests and common pilgrims, and included large numbers of women and children. Just moving them along the same route, controlling them, and ensuring that they were fed and watered would have been a major achievement in itself, but they frequently also had to be defended from brigands, pirates, saracens, and even the hostile local inhabitants of the towns and villages through which they passed. Thus, each of the journeys represented a massive military and logistic undertaking.

In military terms, the crusaders conducted many campaigns, involving both mobile battles and sieges. Sometimes they were defeated, as at Damascus, Hattin and in Egypt, but on other occasions they were successful, as at Acre and Jaffa. Some of their campaigns were complicated, involving the movement of relatively large numbers of troops, horses and equipment by sea, and a few even required opposed landings on arrival. So, despite the many problems, they managed to cooperate with each other for most of the time in the field and in the sieges.

On the other hand, there were many negative aspects. There were, for example, frequent differences between factions, which had a bad enough effect in peacetime but could be disastrous on the battlefield. Sometimes such factions formed on national lines, but on other occasions they centred on the rivalry between the Military Orders, particularly the Hospitallers and Templars. In addition, the people who settled in Outremer often formed factions which fought between themselves, while the later crusaders who arrived for a period of just one or two years viewed all of those who had settled in the Holy Land with profound suspicion, and, of course, vice versa.

One of the more curious factors is the way in which very important people such as kings, dukes and bishops were able to leave their countries for periods varying between one and four years in order to take part in the crusades. They had, of course, to leave somebody to exercise their responsibilities on their behalf, but the lack of communications must have made governance very difficult.

The role of women during this period must not be underestimated. Large numbers of women actually went on the crusades. Eleanor of Aquitaine (then Queen of France) and her train of 300 ladies went on the Second Crusade, while Richard I's wife Berengaria and his sister Joan accompanied the English king on the Third Crusade. Queen Margaret of France accompanied her husband, Louis IX, on the Seventh Crusade, giving birth to a son in the very unpleasant conditions of the camp at Damietta, while simultaneously organising the ransom for her husband who had just been captured. Unfortunately, only the exploits of those at the top of the social tree were deemed worthy of recording, although their adventures were exciting enough; but there were hundreds, if not thousands, of other women lower down the

RIGHT: Peter the Hermit riding an ass as he leads the "People's Crusade". The motives of some involved in the crusades were undoubtedly base, and there were many charlatans, but the majority were driven by their sincerely held religious beliefs and a desire to (as they saw it) free the Holy Land from saracen control. Hundreds of thousands were to perish in pursuit of that goal.

social scale who also accompanied their husbands and who shared to the full the trials and tribulations of crusading, and whose experiences went unrecorded.

Nor was the impact only on those women who went on the crusades, because those who stayed at home, especially wives, were left to run houses and estates, to look after their families and to raise children. Some, such as Queen Eleanor of England, were even left as regents to run kingdoms, and did so rather well.

The expulsion of the crusaders from the Holy Land in 1291 did not end crusading efforts, but the responses of European kings and nobles to further calls to "free" the Holy Land were feeble, and nothing more of note was achieved. Two hundred years of crusades left little long-term mark on the Holy Land, apart from the castles, churches, and fortifications which the crusaders built, many of which remain, in various degrees of preservation, today.

The main effects of the crusades were felt in Europe. The crusades greatly increased the commercial activities of the Italian and other established markets, and this proved to be of enduring importance. The crusades proved to be very expensive undertakings and the novel means used by successive Popes and European monarchs to raise money to finance them were so successful that they led directly to the system of general taxation that is in use today. The crusader states established in the Holy Land lasted only for some two hundred years, but the experience gained subsequently formed the basis of the systems used by Europeans when they began to colonize overseas territories from the 15th Century onwards.

At the start of the crusades the western Europeans were brutal, unsophisticated and militarily inept compared with the sophisticated and civilised societies of Christian Byzantium and the Muslim Middle East. However, the crusaders were by no means immune to what they saw in the Middle East, and when they returned home they passed on at least some of what they had learnt.

BELOW: Eleanor of Aquitaine (1122-1204) was one of the great individuals of the era, a person of tremendous intelligence, drive and courage. In her time, she was Queen of France, then Queen of England, and finally regent during her son Richard's absence on the crusades.

In military terms, such lessons included the art of manoeuvre on the battlefield, the use of light cavalry for reconnaissance, the use of mounted archers to provide mobile firepower, and the need for cavalry (the knights) and infantry to work together. The crusaders also learnt the importance of fortifications and castles, which resulted in a revolution in the design and construction of castles throughout Europe in the 12th and 13th Centuries.

They also learnt the value of logistic support, especially when operating over long distances in hostile territory. Most such lessons were learnt the hard way; for example, it has been estimated that during the First and Second Crusades more men and horses died for lack of food and fodder than from attacks by the saracens. But, the man who was probably the greatest of all crusader generals, Richard the Lionheart, was skilled not only at tactics and leadership, but also had a very clear understanding of logistics.

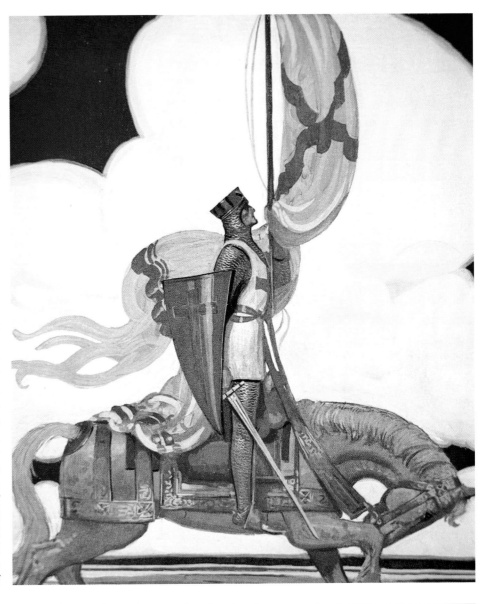

ABOVE: "The Ideal of the Crusades", a symbolic painting by Graham Simmonds. Whatever their shortcomings – and they had many, as this book has shown – the crusaders have left an image of men and women struggling to achieve a great, noble and idealistic goal.

The last of the crusaders may have left the Holy Land in 1291, but the idea, the name, and the imagery have lived on until today. The term "crusade" is still used from time to time to describe undertakings that have a perceived moral purpose. Thus, when the British General Allenby captured Jerusalem in 1917 he was popularly considered to be a latter-day crusader, and was depicted as such in a very popular cartoon in the magazine *Punch* in which he was wore armour and was shown as a reincarnation of the spirit of Richard the Lionheart. Later, during World War II, the British Army named one of its most important tank designs the Crusader, while one of the biggest operations in the Western Desert campaign was given the codename Operation Crusader.

In the early 1950s General Dwight D. Eisenhower, who had been Supreme Allied Commander in Europe during World War II, wrote describing events of the war in a book whose title was *Crusade in Europe*. Slightly later, during the Cold War the United States Navy chose the name "Crusader" for two very successful aircraft, while the new self-propelled gun to be fielded by the US Army over the next few years is also named the "Crusader."

Nor has Western use of terms from this long-gone era been limited to one side. When the British Army introduced two new armoured vehicles in the 1950s and wanted to give them dashing names, symbolising a combination of armoured protection and speed of movement, they saw nothing odd or unusual in naming the personnel carrier the "Saracen" and the armoured car, one of the finest of its era, the "Saladin".

Thus, the names, reputations and aura of both the crusaders and the saracens – who fought each other for so long and such a long time ago – live on.

750-1258	Caliphate of the Abbassids.
868-905	Rule of Talunids in Egypt. Egypt only nominally subject to Caliphate of Abbassids.
969-1171	Rule of Fatimid dynasty in Egypt. Nominal suzerainty of the Abbassids in Egypt is ended.
1016	Norman conquest of Southern Italy begins.
1054	Schism within Christian Church, which then divides into Greek Orthodox and Roman Catholic.
1055	Seljuk Turks capture Baghdad.
1061	Start of Norman conquest of Sicily.
1070	Seljuks take Jerusalem from Fatimids.
1071	Battle of Manzikert. Seljuks under Alp Arslan defeat Byzantine army and found Sultanate of Rum in Asia Minor.
1073-1085	Papacy of Pope Gregory VII.
1074	Pope Gregory VII plans crusade for the support of Byzantium against the Seljuks and to gain dominance of Rome over the Byzantine Church.
1081-1118	Reign of Emperor Alexius I, Comnenus, of Byzantium.
1088-1099	Papacy of Pope Urban II.
1095	Council of Clermont; Pope Urban II issues call for crusade.
1096	Fatimids recapture Jerusalem from Seljuk Turks.
March:	Crusader contingents begin to assemble.
Spring:	"Peasants' Crusade" under Peter the Hermit.
October 6:	"Peasants' Crusade" annihilated at Nicaea.
Autumn:	Godfrey reaches Constantinople.
1096-1102	First Crusade.
1097	Main group of First Crusade reaches Constantinople.
July 1:	Battle of Dorylaeum; crusaders defeat Kilij Arslan.
October 21:	Crusaders lay siege to Antioch.
1098	
June 3:	Antioch is taken. Foundation of Principality of Antioch by Bohemond of Taranto.
1098	Baldwin of Boulogne becomes Lord of Edessa.
1099	
July 15:	Crusaders capture Jerusalem. Godfrey of Bouillon elected first Latin ruler of Jerusalem.
1100	Godfrey dies; leaves the crown to his brother, Baldwin.
July:	Founding of the Kingdom of Jerusalem.
December:	Baldwin crowned first King of Jerusalem.

1101	Crushing defeat of crusaders (French, German, Italian) while crossing Anatolia.
1102-1103	Danish Crusade. King Eric I of Denmark dies in Cyprus.
1104	King Baldwin of Jerusalem captures Acre.
1107-1108	Crusade of Bohemond of Taranto.
1108	September: Bohemond surrenders to the Greeks at Durazzo.
1113	Foundation of the Order of St. John of Jerusalem (Hospitallers).
1115	Foundation of the Order of the Poor Knights of Christ (Templars).
1118	King Baldwin I of Jerusalem is succeeded by his son, Baldwin II.
1124	Crusaders capture Tyre, helped by Venetian fleet.
1125	Peasants revolt in Beirut.
1131	Death of Baldwin II, King of Jerusalem. Succeeded by Fulk of Anjou, husband of Melisende.
1131/32	First nobles' revolt in Kingdom of Jerusalem.
1137	Atabeg (emir) Zangi captures Mosul.
1139	Siege of Damascus by Zangi.
1143	Death of King Fulk in riding accident; succeeded by his son, King Baldwin III.
1144	Zangi captures Edessa; end of crusader state.
1146-1174	Nur ad-Din (Nureddin) ruler of Aleppo, Damascus, Mosul and Mesopotamia.
1147-1149	Second Crusade (King Conrad III and Louis VII).
1148	Louis VII with his wife Eleanor of Aquitaine reach Antioch.
	Louis quarrels with Raymond. Louis takes Eleanor by force to Jerusalem.
	Louis, Conrad III of Germany and Baldwin III attack Damascus. Crusaders suffer humiliating defeat.
1149	July: Raymond of Antioch dies in battle.
1155-1190	Reign of Frederick I Barbarossa, Emperor of the Holy Roman Empire.
1154	Nur ad-Din captures Damascus.
1162	Baldwin III, King of Jerusalem, dies; succeeded by his brother Amalric I.
1171	Saladin, son of the Kurdish leader Eijub, overthrows Fatimid dynasty in Egypt.
1171-1230	Ayyubid dynasty in Egypt.

1172	Henry the Lion, Duke of Saxony, leads crusade.
1174	King Amalric of Jerusalem dies of illness; succeeded by his son, Baldwin IV (aged 13), suffering from leprosy.
1189-1199	Reign of Richard Coeur de Lion, King of England.
1185	After long struggle, Saladin unites Egypt and the territories of Damascus, Aleppo and Mosul into a single kingdom.
	King Baldwin IV of Jerusalem dies; succeeded by his nephew, Baldwin V, aged 8.
1186	King Baldwin V of Jerusalem dies. Sibylla, sister of Baldwin IV, seizes crown, and also crowns her husband, Guy of Lusignan, as king.
1187	
July 4:	Battle of the Horns of Hattin. Saladin inflicts crushing defeat on crusader army.
October 2:	City of Jerusalem falls to Saladin.
1189-1191	King Guy of Jerusalem begins Siege of Acre.
1189-1192	Third Crusade
1190	
June 10:	Frederick Barbarossa drowned in the river Saleph.
October:	Remnants of German crusade reach Acre.
1190-1197	Reign of Henry VI, Holy Roman Emperor.
1191	Richard I of England takes Cyprus from Byzantines.
March:	King Philip of France arrives at Acre.
June:	King Richard I of England arrives at Acre.
July 12:	Richard takes Acre.
1191-1192	Armistice between crusaders and Saladin, leaving crusaders with narrow coastal strip and capital at Acre.
1193	Death of Saladin; his sons dispute their inheritance which is divided among them.
1197	Crusade of Henry VI, Holy Roman Emperor, who dies in Sicily.
1198	King Amalric II of Jerusalem signs five-year treaty with Malik-al-Adil.
1199	Papal charter for Order of Teutonic Knights with main base at Acre.
1198-1216	Papacy of Pope Innocent III.
1202	Fourth Crusade starts with capture of Zara for Venice as the price of their sea passage to the east.
1202-1204	Fourth Crusade, originally planned against Egypt, diverted to Byzantium.
1203	
July 17:	Crusaders capture Constantinople for the first time.

1204	
April 12:	Second capture of Constantinople; crusaders sack the city.
1204-1261	Crusaders establish "Latin Empire of Romania" with Baldwin of Flanders as emperor.
1209-1219	Albigensian crusade, led by Simon de Montfort.
1212	Children's Crusade, the greatest single tragedy in the entire crusading episode.
1215	Fourth Lateran Council.
1217-1229	Fifth Crusade: several expeditions, with Egypt as main objective.
1217-1218	Crusade of King Andrew II of Hungary to capture Acre.
1219-1221	Crusade under Cardinal Pelagius to capture Damietta.
1219	St. Francis of Assisi tries and fails to convert Sultan Al-Kamil to Christianity.
1229-1233	Civil war in Latin Kingdom of Cyprus.
1228-29	Crusade of Holy Roman Emperor Frederick II. Jerusalem returned to crusader states by treaty; Frederick crowned King of Jerusalem in Jerusalem.
1244	Muslims retake Jerusalem; crusader forces defeated at battle of La Forbie (Gaza).
1248-1254	Sixth Crusade. King Louis IX of France captures Damietta, is defeated and taken prisoner. On release he goes to the Holy Land where he remains for four years.
1256-1258	Civil war in Kingdom of Jerusalem.
1259	Baybars defeats Mongols and unites Egypt and Syria.
1260-1277	Reign of Baybars as the Mameluke Sultan of Egypt.
1261	Byzantines retake Constantinople and much of southern Greece; end "Latin Empire of Romania".
1268	Sultan Baybars captures Jaffa and Antioch.
1270	Seventh Crusade, campaign by Louis IX of France against Tunis. Louis dies.
1277-1278	Charles of Anjou buys Kingdom of Jerusalem, takes over Latin principality of Achaea.
1282	Invasion of Italy by Aragonese; start of Angevin-Neapolitan and Aragonese rivalry in eastern Mediterranean.
1286	Kingdom of Jerusalem under King of Cyprus.
1289	Crusaders lose Tripoli.
1291	Last Crusader base, Acre, is lost to Mamelukes under Sultan Al Ashraf.
	End of Kingdom of Jerusalem.
	Crusaders withdraw to Cyprus.

GLOSSARY

GENERAL TERMS

Barbote. Crusader ships fitted with shields to protect archers; for use in sieges.

Connaissances. Heraldic emblems.

Dubbing. Knighting ceremony.

Fief. Piece of land held by a knight.

Indulgence. Certificate given by the Church, forgiving sins in return for a specified penance.

Iqta (A). Fief (*qv*).

Jihad (A). Holy War.

Mahonesi. Association of ship-owners, merchants and/or knights governing Genoese colonial outposts.

Maidan (A). Parade-ground.

Zardkhanah (A). Arsenal.

PEOPLE

Archons. Military elite in Latin Greece.

Askar (A). Soldier.

Baili. Government's military representative.

Castellan. Keeper of castle (see also **Chatelain**).

Chatelain. Keeper of castle (see also **Castellan**).

Connétable. Second ranking royal military officer of state.

Conrois. Unit of cavalry comprising some 20-24 knights.

Faris (A). Cavalryman.

Frank. Originally, a member of one of the Germanic tribes of the Rhine region, but after they conquered Gaul in about 300AD it became a general term for a Frenchman. Used by saracens to describe any European.

Gonfanonier. Standard-bearer.

Halka (A). Elite regiments of Ayyubid army.

Latin. In the context of the crusades "Latin" referred to the Roman Catholic Church as opposed to the Eastern Orthodox Church.

Mameluke (A). A military caste, originally composed of Turkish slaves, who ruled Egypt from about 1250 to 1517.

Maréchal. Third rank of military officer in royal service in crusading armies.

Pursuiviant. New knight, a "learner".

Sénéchal. Senior military government official in crusader armies.

Squire. Knight's servant.

Tawashi. Professional elite cavalryman.

Troubadour. Poet/singer.

Turkoman (A). Turkish tribal nomad.

Turcopoles. Mounted archers, mostly Syrian mercenaries employed by the crusader military orders.

ARMOUR

Ailettes. Shoulder pieces, but for display only.

Aketon. Quilted armour, made of cotton. Adopted by the crusaders from the saracen original, the name being an adaptation of the Arabic original, *al-Q'tun*.

Asergum. See **Hauberk**.

Aventail. Mail attached to the rim of a helmet.

Baldric. A belt, usually made of leather, worn across one shoulder and across the chest to support a sword.

Barberia. Mail **Coif** (*qv*).

Barbuta. Deep form of **Bascinet** (*qv*) with greater face protection.

Bascinet. Helmet covering sides and rear of head, with deep visor.

Besagews. Discs protecting elbow.

Boss. A circular or knob-like protuberance on a shield.

Bras de fer. Early form of arm protection.

Brigandine. Flexible **Cuirass** (*qv*) made of very small plates.

Calicas ferreis. Leg armour.

Caligas. Boots or **Greaves** (*qv*).

Cercle. Lower rim of helmet.

Cervellière. Light hemispherical inner helmet

Chausses. Mail stockings.

Clavain. Neck and shoulder protection.

Clipeum. Shield.

Coat-of-plates. Segmented body armour attached to leather or fabric base.

Coif. Flexible head protection.

Coleriam. Armour for neck and shoulders.

Couter. Armour for elbow.

Cuir-bouilli. Leather soaked and left to harden, used as an early form of armour (Fr. "boiled leather").

Cuirass. Plated body armour to protect both chest and back, or, in some cases, only the chest.

Cuirie. Body armour of buff leather.

Cuisses. Armour for thighs and and knees.

Dir' (A). Hauberk (*qv*).

Ecu (Fr). Shield (from Latin *scutum* = shield).

Enarmes. Holding straps on shield.

Espalière. Shoulder armour.

Faldis spontonem. Armour for abdomen.

Fenestral. Part of helmet protecting face.

Ferro gamberias. Leg armour.

Flamboiant. Piece of coloured cloth on helmet.

Gamberuolis. Leg armour.

Gambeson. Form of soft-armour; quilted.

Gorgèrettes. Neck protection.

Gorgière de plate. Scale-lined **Aventail** (*qv*) or neck protection.

Great helm. Heavy helmet covering entire head.

Greaves. Armour for lower leg.

Guige. Supporting neck strap of shield.

Haubergeon. Short-sleeved mail armour.

Hauberk. Mail shirt or tunic.

Heaume à visière. Helmet with fixed or movable face protection.

Jawshan (A). Body armour of **Lamellar** (*qv*) construction

Jubbah (A). Mail-lined armour.

Jupeau d'armer. Form of padded armour; name *jupeau* is taken from Arabic *jubbah* = quilted armour.

Kazakhand (A). Mail-lined armour.

Lamerias. Early form of **Cuirass** (*qv*).

Lamellar. Armoured protection consisting of small rigid pieces of iron or leather laced together.

Latten. A metal alloy similar to brass.

Manicis cirotecas de ferro. Iron protectors for the arm.

Panceria. Form of **Hauberk** (*qv*).

Pavises. Large, infantry shield.

Pizain. Larger form of **Aventail** (*qv*).

Poleyn. Knee protection.

Pommel. A knob on the hilt of a sword. Also, the raised front part of a horse's saddle.

Rerebrace. Armour protection for for upper arm.

Sabatons. Armoured shoes.

Scabbard. Protective casing for a sword.

Scutum. Shield

Spangenhelm. Helmet

Spur. Metal spike or spiked wheel attached to the heel of a rider's boot and used to urge the horse forward.

Surcoat. Garment worn over armour.

Tabolaccium. Large shield.

Tabolaccium anglum. Shield with angled corners.

Tabolatum. Large shield.

Talevaz. Largest shield.

Targe. Kite-shaped, light shield.

Tippet. Lower end of mail **Coif** (*qv*) covering the shoulders.

Vambrace. Armour protection for lower arm.

Ventail. Flap of mail on **Coif** (*qv*) to protect chin.

Volet. Decorative "veil" tied around helmet.

War-hat. Brimmed helmet.

MAJOR WEAPONS

Ballista. Large crossbow mounted on wooden frame.

Mangana. Large throwing machine.

Mangonel. Smaller version of **Mangana** (*qv*).

Petraria. Stone throwing machine, possibly another name for **Mangana** (*qv*).

Trebuchet. Throwing machine using lever.

Tripantum. Throwing device.

PERSONAL WEAPONS

Baselard. Dagger with H-shaped hilt.

Bow, composite. Bow made of wood, horn and animal sinews.

Couteau. Dagger.

Cultellum de ferro. Dagger.

Graper. Wooden disc around haft of spear.

Hilt. The handle of a sword or dagger.

Lance. A thrusting weapon used by horsemen. It had a long, thin wooden shaft.

Lanceam. Lance (*qv*).

Mace. Heavy metal war club with a spiked or flanged metal head, used for crushing armour in hand-to-hand combat.

Maistre. Summit of helmet.

Misericorde. A long, thin dagger, traditionally used to end the life of a mortally wounded knight (literally, "to have pity").

Mittens. See **Mufflers**.

Mufflers. Mail protection for hands.

Nasal. Metal strip on front of helmet to protect the wearer's nose.

Quillons. The cross-piece on a sword, one quillon sticking out on each side.

Quintaine. Revolving target used in training with lance.

Quiver. Container for arrows, usually carried on the back on a sling.

Spatam. Sword.

Spear. Long weapon carried by knights.

Stocchi. Dagger.

Tang. The long projection from the top of the sword blade to which the handle is secured.

HORSES AND HORSE FURNITURE

Caparison. Horsecloth covering most or all of animal.

Chamfron. Armoured covering for horse's head.

Couvertures. Fabric covering for horse.

Couvertures de fer. Mail horse-armour.

Couvertures de plates. Plated horse armour.

Crupiére. Armour for rear of horse.

Destrier. War horse.

Flanchière. Armour for front and side of horse.

Lorain. Decorative metallic plaques on horse-harness.

Palfrey. Riding horse not used in battle.

Peytral. Breast-strap of horse-harness.

Sumpter. Pack horse.

Tarida (A). Specialised galley for transporting horses.

Testeriam. Head armour for horse.

TACTICAL TERMS

Chevauchée. Raid.

Conrois. Cavalry formation.

Crow. Device for trapping and raising attackers on a siege.

Echelles. Squadrons.

Restor. System whereby the King of Jerusalem replaced the value of horse or military equipment lost when knights served outside the kingdom.

Sap, sapping. In siege warfare, an approach to the walls by engineers using a trench. The trench was open-topped but usually covered by protective wooden covers.

Mine. In siege warfare an approach to under or part of the walls of a castle using a subterranean tunnel.

INDEX